BUSINESS NIGHTMARES

This book is dedicated to my fifth son, Jack,
who was born on 3 October 2007
– my other major creation of 2007.

BUSINESS NIGHTMARES

HITTING ROCK BOTTOM AND COMING OUT ON TOP

Viva Books

New Delhi | Mumbai | Chennai | Kolkata | Bangalore | Hyderabad | Kochi | Guwahati

DISCLAIMER

The advice and observations contained in this book are based on my personal business experience and opinions, but may not be appropriate for your business situation. I would always recommend that you take expert professional advice before moving to action. Neither the publisher nor I can accept responsibility for any loss or consequential damages arising out of any part of this book.

Rachel Elnaugh

First Indian Edition 2010

VIVA BOOKS PRIVATE LIMITED

- 4737/23 Ansari Road, Daryaganj, New Delhi 110 002
  E-mail: vivadelhi@vivagroupindia.net, Tel. 42242200
- 76, Service Industries, Shirvane, Sector 1, Nerul, Navi Mumbai 400 706
  E-mail: vivamumbai@vivagroupindia.net, Tel. 27721273, 27721274
- Jamals Fazal Chambers, 26 Greams Road, Chennai 600 006
  E-mail: vivachennai@vivagroupindia.net, Tel. 28290304, 28294241
- B-103, Jindal Towers, 21/1A/3 Darga Road, Kolkata 700 017
  E-mail: vivakolkata@vivagroupindia.net, Tel. 22836381, 22816713
- 7, Sovereign Park Apartments, 56-58, K. R. Road, Basavanagudi, Bangalore 560 004
  E-mail: vivabangalore@vivagroupindia.net, Tel. 26607409, 26607410
- 101-102 Mughal Marc Apartments, 3-4-637 to 641, Narayanguda, Hyderabad 500 029
  E-mail: vivahyderabad@vivagroupindia.net, Tel. 27564481, 27564482
- Beevi Towers, First Floor, SRM Road, Kaloor, Kochi 682 018, Kerala
  E-mail: vivakochi@vivagroupindia.net, Tel: 0484-2403055, 2403056
- 232, GNB Road, Beside UCO Bank, Silpukhuri, Guwahati 781 003
  E-mail: vivaguwahati@vivagroupindia.net, Tel: 0361-2666386

www.vivagroupindia.com

Published by arrangement with

Crimson Publishing,
a division of Crimson Business Ltd
Westminster House, Kew Road
Richmond, Surrey TW9 2ND

ISBN : 978-81-309-1519-7

Published by Vinod Vasishtha for Viva Books Private Limited, 4737/23, Ansari Road, Daryaganj, New Delhi - 110 002.

Printed and bound by Raj Press, R-3, Inderpuri, New Delhi - 110 012.

CONTENTS

INTRODUCTION

Despite the title *Business Nightmares*, I always intended this to be a very positive business book, since it is not only about problems in business (there will always be problems in business) but crucially about how those problems were overcome. The stories here, all about self-made entrepreneurs, illustrate that amazing things can ultimately emerge from times of great business struggle.

Every entrepreneur I have written about in these pages is incredibly successful, and yet each has encountered serious trials and setbacks during their business journey. In researching this book, it became clear to me that there isn't a business-person alive who has had an entirely smooth ride. In fact, I would venture to suggest that it is actually adversity itself which is the catalyst that hardens those who are tough enough to survive it from being just business wannabes, to becoming the most brilliant entrepreneurs of our age.

I was originally inspired to write this book by the many entrepreneurs who confided in me about their own problems in business following the meltdown of my own company Red Letter Days in 2005.

When the end finally came (and bear in mind I had just given birth to my fourth son a week before; a priceless consolation if ever there was one), instead of the anticipated depression of 'losing it all', I actually felt a huge liberation; I was free of the struggle, and, at last, didn't have to get up and go into battle every day. It's surprising what we cling to in life for so long, when in fact what we should be doing is simply letting go.

When I did finally 'let go', the most amazing things started to happen. Along with all sorts of new opportunities and offers came a whole stream of messages of support completely out of the blue, many of them from other high-profile entrepreneurs, sharing with me their own nightmare business experiences that they had endured along the way. Stories that had been carefully played out behind the scenes and kept out of the press, from people who I had previously (mistakenly) thought had enjoyed a one-way ticket to success, without any of the struggle I had gone through. If only I had known and could have spoken to those people when I was going through my problems, perhaps everything would have turned out differently.

It occurred to me that this was a huge problem in the way business is reported – particularly in the UK. The successes and the glories are all played up to maximise the positive PR, while the real problems and struggles are swept under the carpet. The modern-day media love the 'rags to riches' business fairytale story. So when entrepreneurs start to hit problems in their own business journeys, they start to think they are doing something terribly wrong.

The fact is that business is a learning experience from day one – there is no point at which you can actually sit back and relax, free from problems and worries. There are issues to be dealt with and often serious crises to manage every step of the way, no matter what stage you are at. Crucially, those challenges are actually a vital part of the excitement of being an entrepreneur.

So I decided to write this book to explode the myth that business is all plain sailing. I asked some of the biggest names in business to share their experiences with me, and how they overcame the business nightmares they encountered.

Of course, writing this book was not all plain sailing either – and I was staggered at how many people didn't even bother to reply to my requests, let alone agree to spare the time to be interviewed or to put together a response. But I've come to realise that there are lots of reasons why people won't talk about their negative experiences. Quite apart from wanting to keep their PR positive, there is also the fear of legal action from implicated parties, especially where a problem has been resolved by way of a compromise agreement that stipulates absolute confidentiality.

But perseverance pays, and I would like to thank all those who did agree to be part of the project, for both their time and their openness and honesty. When I interviewed the entrepreneurs, I went in with a completely open agenda, and didn't know what insights they would share with me. As it turns out, they have all had some crisis moments.

In the UK there is still a deep-seated dislike and even disgrace attached to failure and (unlike in the USA, where failure is 'de rigueur') people are still ashamed to talk about any mistakes they may have made on their business journey. But in my view it is key that entrepreneurs talk about the problems – if only to give hope and insight to those less-experienced entrepreneurs who are at the earlier stages of their business journey and find themselves struggling, worrying that they are doing something wrong.

Business is anything but easy. Recent research by NatWest bank suggests that, as a result of the spate of successful business TV shows like *Dragons' Den* and *The Apprentice*, there are 17 million people in the UK who are currently considering starting their own business; out of these, 30% intend to act on their idea within the next 12 months. That's 5.1 million new businesses, of which (and I hate to say it) two thirds – 3.4 million – are statistically doomed to fail within their first two years of trading. The majority of the surviving 1.7 million will barely keep their heads above water, their owners spending every waking hour to scratch a living, for less than the minimum wage. Less than 5% (about 250,000) will actually achieve anything amounting to real material success.

So, if you are in business and things are currently looking very dark – times when the shit has hit the fan, those sleepless 3am 'dark night of the soul' moments are all too frequent, and success or failure seems to balance on a knife edge – take heart from the fact that you are amongst the majority, not the minority, and that you are most definitely not alone.

Many great entrepreneurs before you have experienced the same pain. My aim has been to write a book from which all budding entrepreneurs can take heart, strength, encouragement and perhaps some sage advice for the difficult times on their own business journey. Indeed, this book tells of how entrepreneurs before you actually managed to turn disastrous situations to their advantage.

As you will discover from this book, miracles do often happen when you have a little faith, and if you persevere. No matter how terrible things seem, there is always hope on the horizon.

MY STORY SO FAR

I always knew when I was growing up above my dad's electrical shop in Chelmsford, Essex, that one day I would run my own business. While other girls were out playing with their friends during the school holidays, I was down in dad's shop, sitting at the cashier's desk counting the money, or sorting out the light bulbs into a neat order.

Every Christmas my mum and I would set up a little table in the shop from which we would sell homemade crackers, gift tags made from old Christmas cards and various other seasonal paraphernalia, all in aid of charity. Every time we made a sale it was hugely exciting to me, like a little piece of gratification, a bit of positive feedback, and a clue to what the customer wanted to buy. I was starting to get hooked on ways to sell more and more. So I turned up production on the most successful cracker colours and phased out the ones no one wanted.

Much of my childhood was spent with my mum at various wholesalers and manufacturers, buying paper, packaging, novelties and various off-cuts, which we could somehow use to make things to sell on our Christmas table. We would spray twisted willow silver and attach tiny baubles for table ornaments. Everything we sold went into Christmas bags that I had made.

I would also be assigned to various tasks to help my mum with my dad's business administration, like folding invoices to go into envelopes and sticking the stamps on ready to post. When I was a bit older, I started helping with the accounts and bookkeeping, managing the client ledger and sending out reminders to people who hadn't paid.

I had all sorts of career ideas when I was at school – I wanted to become a journalist, an astrologer, and work in the art world. Being an entrepreneur was never on the radar of the career options at school and so at first I embarked on the traditional route that was expected of me by the girls' grammar school I went to, and I applied to university to study history of art.

Having received rejections from all the universities concerned (not least because I subsequently found out that my headmistress had written on my UCCA form that I 'excelled at mathematics'), I decided to start applying for management training courses instead. Rejection letter after rejection letter followed (and that was from those companies that actually bothered to reply to my feeble applications). In fact I received so many rejection letters I could have wallpapered my bedroom with them. Although I didn't realise it at the time, I was already receiving my first lesson in business – how to keep going despite rejection.

Eventually, in desperation, I replied to a little advert in the local paper asking for an office junior to work in a local firm of accountants for just £2,750 per year. My experience working in my dad's business clinched it for me, and when I received the offer letter I was the happiest girl in the world. Someone actually wanted me at last!

So I got my foot on the ladder and worked my way up from doing the filing and making coffee to doing tax returns for wealthy individuals and small-business owners.

I took my taxation exams by correspondence course and eventually ventured up to the City, where I landed a job specialising in the taxation of Lloyd's Underwriters. This was the time of the PCW scandals at Lloyd's, and even though I hated every moment that I spent at that firm (thanks mainly to a bitch of a boss, who made my time there a living hell through consistent and relentless criticism of everything I did), the experience I gained helped me get a much better role at Arthur Andersen, which was at the time the biggest accountancy firm in the world.

Those two and a half years I spent at Andersen's in my early twenties were probably the most important work experience of my life. They taught me the value of thinking big, and they also introduced me to the world of fabulously wealthy clients, including the entrepreneurs Sir Terence Conran and Anna Vinton who founded Reject Shop. I have always been in awe of celebrities (maybe it's because I'm an Essex girl), but it was a real thrill getting into the lift and finding yourself alongside someone really famous like Bryan Ferry or Joan Collins, who were among Andersen's clients at the time.

The training was international and I got to meet some amazing people and travel to some fantastic places. While the 'OK-yah' Oxbridge graduates stuck to their own London office colleagues, I was the Essex-girl outsider – and so made the effort to get to know all the international delegates.

I'll never forget one of the partners inviting me along to an evening with one of my clients, the entrepreneur Robert Breare. We started off with cocktails at The Savoy, more drinks at Trader Vic's and then dinner at Brian Turner's restaurant in Mayfair, where the chef came out and spoke to Robert personally. I was so young, gauche and nervous, and also pathetically out of my depth, but I knew that this was the life that I was destined for. I knew, from that point onwards, that whatever business I would eventually set up and run would need to be BIG. I later met Robert again when he was judging the Ernst & Young Entrepreneur of the Year Awards in 2002 – he recognised me from over a decade before and I think my transformation impressed him so much it swung it for me to win an award that year.

This was the 1980s and at the time the City was overflowing with money and champagne. It was a fantastically decadent decade. Crucially, it was also the start of the rise of the female entrepreneur. People like Dame Anita Roddick, Debbie Moore and Sophie Mirman were floating their companies on the stock market, and leading the charge for female power was the Iron Lady herself, Margaret Thatcher, who was, and still is, my greatest idol.

By the age of 24 I knew that a career in taxation was not for me, and although I was on course to earn a fantastic salary, I knew in my heart I had to leave Andersen's and free my life up for something new to happen.

So I resigned and set off to hitchhike across Europe with my then lodger, Bill who had just been sacked from his job as security guard at Asprey's for pilfering items from their stock.

We started out in a lay-by on the A12 with just a small amount of money. Our ambition was to visit a friend we knew in Crete. Again, a brilliant entrepreneurial training, negotiating your way across a continent on a shoestring budget by hitching lifts with anyone who will offer them, and getting to know the best techniques to get rides. We reached our destination five days later on a total outlay of less than £100. It was great fun and for the first time in my life I really experienced freedom.

When we finally got home we decided to use our new-found experience as travellers to do the same thing in America. But we had heard that hitchhiking in the USA was extremely dangerous, so we decided to travel by car instead. I rented out my little London flat for six months and we flew to New York, hired a car and drove the 3,000 miles across the southern states to San Francisco, where Bill's sister was on a work experience programme. We slept in the car most nights and once or twice a week stayed in a cheap motel so we could at least shower. But America felt far more dangerous than Europe and I was glad when we finally arrived at our destination. Although we planned to spend six months in America, after six weeks I was bored, and itching to come home and get on with something concrete. My grandmother had also died while I was away and I felt terrible that I could not be there for her funeral.

So, I got back to the UK and, because my flat was still rented out, I started lodging with another friend, Scott McRae, who lived in a warehouse apartment by the River Thames at Rotherhithe. I took a freelance job doing taxation to make ends meet and decided that now would be the time for me to go into business.

The dream

At the time, my brother's girlfriend Sabina was also at a loose end, and so we decided to go into business together. It just felt much safer that way and, rather ridiculously, we ended up doing everything together. We didn't really know what business we wanted to do but I had the urge to do something around gifting – possibly because of all those years doing the Christmas table in my dad's shop, and generally because I had always had a passion for finding unusual presents for people. Sabina started talking about opening a shop in Chelmsford to sell gifts and deliver chocolates and champagne, but that sounded too boring and parochial to me. I was still thinking much bigger, and thought that mail order would be a much better route to market.

At around that time, it was my dad's birthday and he was incredibly difficult to buy for. His passion was cricket and so I decided to buy him tickets to see England play India at Lord's Cricket Ground. As the match was some months away, the tickets weren't issued until a few weeks before the game, and so my challenge was to create a present which I could give him on his birthday, even though I had nothing physically to give. So I created a box of 'clues' – a jar of English mustard, a pot of curry powder, a cricket ball and finally a handwritten invitation. And he loved it!

At about the same time, one of the clients I was asked to work on in my freelancing role was a company called

Scrooge and Marley. They had created a range of 'gift cards' for a variety of activities like motor racing at Brands Hatch, balloon trips, gliding and so on. The idea was that you bought the card for £1 (the proceeds of which went in their entirety to the retailer as the incentive to stock the cards), and inside was an 'activation' card which you sent off with your money to Scrooge and Marley. You then gave the card as your present and the recipient would contact Scrooge and Marley to arrange the activity.

It was a rather clunky procedure, and the cards were badly designed in grim, dark brown, presumably because they couldn't afford to print them in colour. I also knew from the company's paperwork that the business was struggling.

So I guess you could say that I stole the idea for my business, Red Letter Days, from someone else, but it was actually a combination of those two things that provided me with a vision of how I could make the concept work much better. We would create a range of experiences as brilliant gifts for the 'man who had everything' – and work out a way to 'wrap' them beautifully.

In excitement, I went home that night to tell Scott all about my idea. He happened to be a writer for the big creative agency Imagination and, quite without me asking, came back from work the next day with a list of different names for my company; names like 'Wishing Well' and 'Dreams Come True'. On the list was also 'Red Letter Days'.

In an instant I knew that the name was perfect for my business. Not only did it sum up the 'experiences' I was going to offer, it also gave me the ready-made idea for packaging the gifts – a red letter envelope. I always think that your fastest, most instinctive decisions in business – and in life – are your best ones.

This was on 4 July 1989, and out of the window of Scott's warehouse apartment we could see fireworks going off over Tower Bridge, which I took to be a good omen. So the next day I went down to the City to a company formation agent (this was long before you could do it online), and on 5 July 1989 Red Letter Days was born.

Interestingly, not long afterwards, Scrooge and Marley crashed into administration leaving hundreds of customers with worthless gift cards, although many of the suppliers concerned honoured the experiences involved. But the numbers were in the hundreds, not the thousands, and the failure of the company passed almost without notice.

I never told anyone about Scrooge and Marley during the years of Red Letter Days success, but I guess stealing someone else's idea is always, ultimately, going to bring with it bad karma. However, I would still argue to this day that success in business is 1% about the idea and 99% about the execution.

The first task for Sabina and me in Red Letter Days was to create our range of 'experiences' – and of course I thought it was going to be easy. But practically everyone we approached just didn't want to know. They had never heard of the concept before, apart from the few people who'd dealt with Scrooge and Marley and got their fingers burned. I was young and female and I don't think anyone had much confidence that I would actually make my idea a success.

When I started out I was very naive, but by encountering so much hostility and rudeness during those first months and years I soon hardened up. There were people who would say ‘hold the line for a second, I’ll get someone to speak to you’ and then just leave the phone on the desk, leaving you waiting for ages until you realised they had no desire to speak to you, and so you just had to hang up.

Then there were the people like Bob Payton who owned the country house hotel Stapleford Park. I’d written to him asking him to be involved, and then when I received no reply, went to see him at a trade show where he was exhibiting. He told me in no uncertain terms to ‘bugger off’ so he could deal with ‘proper customers’. Charming behaviour from someone in the hospitality industry! I noticed a small piece in the paper a few years later saying that he had died in a car crash on the country roads near his hotel. Interestingly, every person or company who was abusive to me in those early years later either went out of business or came to a sticky end. I guess what goes around comes around, but it made me aware that in business when people are struggling they will often take it out on you.

One of the worst companies to deal with was probably Brands Hatch – burned by their dealings with Scrooge and Marley, they refused to speak to me in year one, and only later in year two did they agree to let us promote one of their least-popular products – parascending – on a commission of just 10%. But I agreed just so I could prove myself to them, and it was only in year three that we finally managed to get them to agree to let us offer their full range. Red Letter Days later went on to become

Brands Hatch's biggest corporate client, spending well over a million pounds a year with them. Talk about lack of vision from the person who initially rejected us (more on this in Chapter 16).

But it wasn't just getting suppliers on board that was a problem. I had seriously underestimated just how difficult it would be to market the business, and stupidly wasted £25,000 on advertising that just didn't work.

Six months into the business, we had just a handful of 'experiences', we had only managed to turn over £10,000, and we had literally no money left.

Sabina seemed disheartened when she realised she was not going to become a millionaire overnight, and her enthusiasm seemed to evaporate (more on that in Chapter 14). I felt like it was pretty much left to me to work out a way to keep going in the face of huge negativity and the well-meaning 'Why don't you go back to accountancy? You'll make far more money' type of comments from friends and family.

I had invested every last penny I had and sold all my possessions to get the business off the ground and absolutely nothing was working. Only those who have been through this business nightmare, which is known as 'the pit', will know how awful those early days can be. Days when the phone doesn't ring a single time, no one will return your calls and you experience nothing but rejection. It takes extraordinary determination and persistence to keep going (see Chapter 13). But I was determined not to give up.

At the time I was still freelancing and I confided in my boss Barrie Dunning (who now handles my taxation affairs) that I knew I had a great idea in Red Letter Days but I just couldn't seem to make it work. Barrie referred me to one of his clients, a designer called Barry Davis who was also an expert in marketing.

Eagerly, I gathered up our first brochure and our first adverts and went to see Barry, hoping he would tell me that all was well with the business. But he just sat there very quietly, shaking his head for what seemed like an eternity, before saying, 'Rachel, I'm sorry but you've wasted your money'.

My heart sank and I felt like crying, but luckily Barry agreed to take me under his wing. He redesigned my clunky brochure into a simple fold-out poster of just 20 experience ideas and on his advice we put it as an insert into *YOU* magazine, a supplement in the *Mail on Sunday*, and *The Daily Telegraph* magazine in the first week of December 1990. We could only afford to print 100,000 copies and to do that I had to persuade my first husband to put up the money. Compared to the circulation of those two magazines, 100,000 inserts is a ludicrously tiny amount, so we had to opt for just one county. We chose Surrey, not because of any market research we had done, but simply because we thought that people in Surrey have money!

From the moment our insert landed on breakfast tables that weekend, the phones didn't stop ringing. So much so that a lot of the calls went unanswered – I had lost hope in the business by that point and was manning two phones by myself in a spare room at home. It was a classic example of over-trading.

Despite this, we managed to take £30,000 in the three weeks leading up to Christmas, which was enough money to kick-start the business. Crucially, we now had proof that this business could actually work.

When a business turns the corner it is amazing just how quickly things can snowball. The suppliers that wouldn't even talk to me for the previous 18 months saw the insert and were now ringing me asking if they could get involved; the people who had received a Red Letter Day for Christmas were also on the phone asking for our brochure so that they could order for other people.

After that, the company mushroomed, almost as if it was out of control. (In fact, at times I have to admit it *was* out of control – although that was actually part of the adrenalin of the ride.) We simply ran with every big opportunity that knocked at the door (we never seemed to chase them) and as a result grew bigger than any well-structured and logically thought through business plan could ever have predicted.

The business started to take over our home, with phones ringing day and night, sacks of mail in the hallway and brochures spilling out of every cupboard. I was also doing everything myself: opening the post in the morning, answering the phone all day, processing all the orders and taking everything to the post office at night.

Every day my first husband, Lax, would come home from work in the City and spend all evening working on the financial side of the business as well as spending hours phoning through all the credit card orders for authorisation (there was no such thing as Streamline machines in those days).

In 1992 (at my insistence – my husband was very much against taking on any overhead) we took our first

550sq ft office in North Finchley. That isn't a huge space as offices go, but it felt like it when it was just me and eight empty second-hand desks. It seemed like a huge indulgence after my cramped desk in our front room, but we soon started to recruit staff and by the end of that year we had a small but happy band of workers.

The next major breakthrough (again on Barry's advice) was to hire a brilliant freelance journalist called Jane Burton who managed to get us coverage in every major women's magazine that Christmas. I had been so badly burned by our experiences in year one (when we ended up dumping thousands of our obsolete brochure) that I refused to print more brochures than I thought were absolutely necessary. As a result, our 1992 brochure *Memories Last Forever* went through at least five reprints and we ended up dispatching over 100,000 copies.

I vividly recall popping into the office one Saturday morning to collect something and noticing that all the phones were constantly ringing. Thinking someone had forgotten to switch on the answering machines the night before, I angrily checked the machines only to find all the tapes were full, so I started answering the phones myself. I ended up sitting there for the whole day fielding call after call – we'd only been featured in the *Daily Mail's* 'Femail' page in a small article called 'How To Make Someone's Day'! That tiny article resulted in well over 3,000 brochure requests alone, and it was then that I truly understood the power of PR.

By this point money was pouring in and turnover had shot up to £300,000. All our systems were still pretty manual but it was clear we needed to find a faster, more efficient way of handling all the orders. I was also a bit of a control freak and insisted on checking and personally signing every single Red Letter before it went out of the office – an activity which consumed at least two hours of my time every day.

Then there were the 'strange requests', like the time a man from Muswell Hill called to ask if we could arrange a breakfast tray to be delivered for his wife's 40th birthday that Saturday morning. Of course when you are an entrepreneur the answer as far as taking orders is concerned is always 'yes', although I charged him the ridiculously low sum of £29 and spent a huge amount of time shopping for and personally delivering the breakfast tray myself. I guess delegation was never my strong point! And of course you learn by experience that it is just not worth taking on projects unless they make you a profit – goodwill is only worth so much.

I was also terribly naive and also a bit stupid. It took £25,000 worth of purchase orders received over a period of six months from electronics giant AEG to start me wondering why they were ordering so many Red Letter Day experiences. When I eventually called them I realised they were using them as a sales incentive scheme, and it was only then that I realised that we had a huge opportunity in the corporate market, which subsequently became the jewel in the company's crown.

My first realisation that the company really had to 'grow up', though, was when we took advantage of a DTI-funded marketing review of our business in around 1993. The consultant (Suzanne Audras) took one look at the pile of Red Letters for signing on my desk and said, 'Just how long do you think you can go on like this?' Of course she was right, and that was the first stage in moving towards a more organised business, even though the prospect of adding the necessary overhead and additional staff seemed a bit scary.

As the company flourished, my relationship with my first husband seemed to deteriorate. He was an Indian and in his family the men very much ruled the roost. When we went to dinner at his family's houses the women always stayed in the kitchen and cooked the chapattis while the men sat together and talked business. Yet my success was starting to eclipse everyone in his family, and my husband was still working in corporate finance in the City, even though he longed to run a business of his own. I spent more and more time working at Red Letter Days and less and less time at home.

Eventually, under the pressure of it all, in 1995 we decided to separate. That was a terribly lonely and depressing time for me and I threw myself into an exercise regime as my way of coping. At one point I was doing eight hours of exercise a week and was probably the fittest I have ever been in my life!

It was at this point that I met my personal fitness trainer at the gym. He started to give me one-to-one lessons in self-defence and one day, quite to my surprise, he asked me out. I was so nervous going on that first date – having been out of the dating loop for probably a decade – but it led to a five-year relationship by which I had my first and second sons.

Having gone through a hideous divorce I was really in no hurry to get married again, and in any event I thought I was perfectly self-sufficient in every respect and didn't really need a man. So when my first baby arrived in 1996 it was a huge shock to the system, and I quickly realised I couldn't cope.

My ex-husband was still part of the business and we agreed that he would take over as managing director and I would focus on marketing, which was the area of the business I loved most. I also managed to find a brilliant childminder called Beryl Broadhurst, who virtually became a surrogate mother to my first two children and without whom I don't think I could have made it through as a career woman as well as a single mum.

At that point Red Letter Days' turnover was £1.2 million, and by focusing on developing the brand, things quickly started to take off. I brought in some market research specialists, who replaced my gut instinct with some real insights, and it was as a result of sitting behind the one-way glass watching those focus groups that I realised we had an opportunity to develop Red Letter Days into something really big. At this time I met Paul Glyde, a copywriter and advertising guru, who became one of my most influential mentors.

It was Paul who taught me a huge amount about marketing and the importance of selling 'the sizzle', not the sausage. I realised through working with Paul that Red Letter Days didn't actually sell motor racing days or balloon flights or health spa weekends at all! What we actually sold was the power to make someone happy, and it was that emotional connection which became the cornerstone of all our marketing and brand development from that moment on.

We worked hard at making our brochure an inspirational read and something that customers would want to keep on their coffee table. It was a good strategy because people would only have two or three special occasions a year that might warrant a Red Letter Day gift, so it was essential that our marketing collateral was 'keepable'. We also deliberately went out to find 'ultimate experiences', like our $20million trip into space. Of course we never sold a single one – but the PR we obtained sold a lot of £99 vouchers!

We were also the first company to deploy variable digital print technology, which allowed us to produce any number of different Red Letter Packs with no need to produce any printed stock of contents, allowing us to scale up our experience range to the point where we had over 4,000 experience permutations. It was the kind of innovation that kept us racing ahead of the many competitors who were starting to emerge on the scene.

By 1998 business was booming, but disaster struck. Lax had taken the view that many of the operational controls (which I had actually put in place as a result of earlier operational issues when we were much smaller) could be scaled back (I think he probably thought that I was obsessed with perfection). Unfortunately events proved they were still needed. Our customers would be turning up at experiences and the supplier would have received no confirmation, so had not reserved a place for them, or the venue would be expecting someone who was booked but the customer did not show because we'd forgotten to send them a letter. Pretty soon we were starting to piss off a lot of people, and it took just seven letters of complaint to BBC TV's *Watchdog* programme to get us featured on the show.

This was at the time when *Watchdog* was at the peak of its power and was presented by the formidable Anne

Robinson. We called an emergency meeting of all our advisers and I was told in no uncertain terms that I would have to go on television and face the music. I was four months pregnant with my second son at the time and was so terrified at the prospect that I had to leave the meeting to be sick and was taken home, throwing up all the way. But we brought in a brilliant media advisor, John Swinfield, who gave me an entire day's media training to prepare me for the ordeal, and on 30 October 1998 I endured my first live TV experience.

It actually turned out to be something of a triumph, and when I returned to the office that evening (everyone had chosen to stay to watch the show and to man the phones in case the show generated any calls), the whole team cheered – and I broke down in tears.

That was a watershed moment for the business, and we all made the decision that we would take our foot off the marketing accelerator and focus on getting our systems back in order. I then spent three months personally running the customer complaints department (it was actually called 'customer care' but all they ever did was field angry calls and letters) and it became apparent just how great was the mess that had to be cleared up.

As I said earlier, Red Letter Days was a business sold on emotion, and boy, did people get angry if you messed up their special birthday! Making mistakes was just not an option for the company, although we never did get to the stage where the business was absolutely complaint free.

After three years at the helm, I think Lax realised that running a business was far from easy. He seemed particularly embarrassed of the fact that while turnover had grown, thanks to all the inefficiencies in the new system, profitability had actually dropped. Eventually my co-director Richard Kaffel and I agreed to buy his 40% stake for £500,000.

The deal was completed on 6 April 2000 and Lax flew to the Cayman Islands to receive the money tax free, flying on to create a new life for himself in New York. I never saw him again.

By the time Lax sold out, turnover was £5 million and we started to be approached by retailers, whose research had shown that 'experiences' were the biggest consumer trend in gifting, and who wanted to get in on the act. The first major retailer was Boots, who painted a vision of working in partnership with us over a five-year period to create a gift experiences range – a deal that would be worth millions. But I soon learned that I was entering another shark-infested pond and would need to harden up even further: after eagerly divulging all our trade secrets of what worked and what didn't, in year two we were cut out of the loop and Boots started to work directly with our suppliers. We had trusted them, and had not thought to tie them into a formal five-year contract. It seems there are no ethics in big business, and particularly none where retail buyers are concerned. You live and learn.

(Interestingly a few years later, burdened by the sheer weight of the administration that went with servicing their gift experiences range in house, Boots invited us to pitch for the entire contract, an offer which we took great pleasure in rejecting. There is precious little money to be made in white label retail contracts, as our competitors soon found.)

The Boots deal led to other much more lucrative projects, in particular with the department store Debenhams. Our exclusive branded range of gift boxes, which we launched in November 2000, sold phenomenally well, and soon Debenhams were spending millions of pounds a year with us. Turnover quickly doubled, and we were subsequently approached by a whole variety of retailers to create ranges for them – from Harrods to Homebase and everyone in between.

(Funnily enough we heard a while later that the buyer who dealt with our first Debenhams range ended up at BHS and at the first buying meeting tried to suggest that they should stock our products. However, BHS had unsuccessfully tried to sell our competitor Activity Superstore's products a year earlier, and it was Philip Green himself who blocked the suggestion by thundering, 'Experiences don't work in retail!' It just serves to illustrate how powerful it is to own the market-leading brand in a sector.)

We quickly realised that we needed to develop our experiences so they could sit alongside other premium gift brands like Sony, Gucci and Tiffany. Our market research uncovered that customers loved the Red Letter Days pack, in fact it was found to be our most valuable piece of brand collateral, and symbolic of a brilliant experience in much the same way that the blue Tiffany box is iconic for jewellery.

My marketing manager at the time, Simon Brenner, really wanted to invest some money making the pack incredibly special. I thought it was a great idea and asked him whom he was planning to use. He had seen Richard Seymour on Channel 4's show *Better by Design,* who was famous for creating the Bioform Bra and said, 'Wouldn't it be great if we could get that guy to design our pack?' To which I said, 'Go for it!' and luckily Richard agreed to take the project on. It cost £100,000, but the investment was well worth it, yielding £5million in orders that year from Debenhams alone.

By that point, the company had been profitable and successful for well over a decade, the staff were like a family to me and it was all great fun. Our growth was entirely organic, and looking back, I now realise that this is by far the safest way to grow a business, even if it does take a little longer than throwing massive resources, in to accelerate turnover.

The work we had done to get the company back into shape paid off, and in 2001 we achieved a profit of £1million on £10million turnover. The dividends from this were alone enough to repay the money I had borrowed to buy Lax's shares. Everything was very rosy indeed – and I was even starting to win business awards for my success.

My Business Nightmare

However, in reality, Red Letter Days was starting to buckle under the strain of so much business. Our operating software was useless and we couldn't even identify which customers had ordered more than once from us. Our accounting was also a mess and we didn't know exactly what our liabilities were on vouchers issued.

The temptation was to take on all of the new retail business (when you have struggled so much to build a business it is very difficult to turn opportunities down), but I knew there was no way that we could take on all the projects we were being offered. Having endured the *Watchdog* ordeal and my TV baptism of fire, I desperately did not want to allow the company to get back into that situation.

At about this time, I was sent an invitation to a lunch with our PR agency, Shandwick, where the guest was the new producer of *Watchdog*, so I decided to accept, with the idea that I would cosy up to the producer and bring him onside should any unfortunate incidents unfold which might cause us to be featured again.

In fact, the lunch resulted in a different outcome. The person whom I was seated next to happened to be a management consultant, and as I explained my business to him and some of the challenges we were facing, he suggested that his consultancy might be able to help. So I commissioned them to do a marketing and brand strategy review, which eventually turned into a full business review.

When the board sat down for the final presentation in March 2002, the outcome was predictable. The consultants told us that the time had come for the business to 'grow up' – to bring in some structure and to formalise its plans. There was also the small matter of 30 projects that needed to be implemented as a result of the review, projects which would transform our business in every area – from our marketing and operations to our systems and management information.

It all sounded very sensible and seemed logical, so when the consultants also suggested to me that perhaps the time had come to put in a 'proper CEO', I agreed that they were probably right. After all, I'd taken the business from nothing to a £14million turnover by that point; I had no real business training and I probably didn't actually know what I was doing anyway. Maybe it had all been just a fluke. A crisis of confidence, which I will explain more about in Chapter 3.

So I recruited a new CEO and stepped back into a non-executive chairman role. This was a fatal mistake, which I have since learned that many entrepreneurs before me have also made to their cost – although at the time it seemed the right thing to do, particularly as I was having so much fun gladding it up at awards ceremonies and being courted by the BBC, who wanted me to take part in a new TV show called *The Bunker* in which I would have to run the country as part of a team of three as a crisis unfolded live around us.

The writing should have been on the wall, as our team in the programme managed to allow a jumbo jet to crash into the Houses of Parliament, rupturing the tube tunnel underneath Westminster and killing 4,000 people who were trapped in the London Underground in the ensuing flood. It took me years to get on a tube train again! That year was also the beginning of the end for Red Letter Days.

The business over expanded and over spent. We lost all our great innovative 'right-brain' entrepreneurial marketing people in favour of an army of project managers and other 'left-brain' types – who were so busy writing 28-page Project Initiation Documents and Gant charts that they barely noticed that the business had customers. Plus the board had management information that was both inadequate and inaccurate.

In little more than a year the business plunged from making a million-pound profit a year to sustaining a loss of £4.7million in the year to 31 July 2003. In business terms, this is like having a hole blown in the side of the ship.

So many people told me to just dump the business at that stage (I had no personal guarantees to defend), but I knew that I would never forgive myself if I did not do everything I possibly could to try to save my baby.

I was seven months pregnant with my third child at the time but I rented a flat in London where I could stay during the week and worked around the clock to try to bring things back on track, stopping the haemorrhage of cash and stripping out a lot of the overhead which had been built in.

By the end of 2003 it looked as if things were going to be OK and it was at that point that I was approached by the BBC, who were recruiting for a new business show called *Dragons' Den*. The producer was the same guy I had worked with on *The Bunker* and had obviously been impressed by my on-screen performance. (I'm still not sure why, as I made such a total cock-up of things, but then cock-ups make great television!) We filmed the pilot in March 2004 and the main part of the first series that autumn. That first show was great fun to shoot and it started to become clear that we had a hit on our hands.

Dragons' Den

I believe that the casting of the original five Dragons by the genius original director Martyn Smith, was key to the huge cult success of *Dragons' Den*.

The only 'Dragon' who I had met before was Simon Woodroffe, the flamboyant founder of Yo! Sushi, who had interviewed me for a TV pilot show a year or so before. Simon already had lots of TV experience, was hugely entertaining and had also mastered the 'art of the soundbite' – so his presence really lifted the whole show. We quickly learned a lot from him about how to make business interesting. Amusingly, during the filming of series 2, when Simon had been changed in favour of Theo Paphitis, one of the producers came up to me between takes and said 'Rachel, we need to bring out the human side of the entrepreneurs and we need some more fun', expecting me to be the one to do it. To which I replied: 'Then you should have kept Simon on the show'.

Dragon Duncan Bannatyne was probably the most ruggedly attractive and successful of all the Dragons. He'd clawed his way up from his first business as an ice cream van man to become founder of Bannatyne Fitness and all things 'Bannatyne' – including a hotel and a casino. Duncan had a great down to earth common sense, called a spade a spade, and although quite hard, was incredibly charming with it. Duncan attracted women like bees to honey and his mobile phone was always hot with messages and texts during filming while I was there.

At the centre of the Dragons – and I believe the heart of the show – we had Doug Richard, whose brain was like a Pentium Core computer on acid, and who could laser straight to the heart of any business model, exploding the issues (and often the entrepreneurs with it) within seconds! If it hadn't been for Doug the show would not have been nearly so interesting or edgy, and I think *Dragons' Den* lost a lot of its uniqueness when Doug left the panel.

And finally, the tall, dark and handsome Peter Jones, who often sat very quietly at the end of the panel just absorbing all the information and coming out with a really well rounded summary of the business and why he would or wouldn't be investing. He was such a well-mannered gentleman in every respect, it would be very easy for a damsel in distress to believe that he would be the knight in shining armour who would come to her rescue.

I was of course always the 'gratuitous female' on the show, and although I gave my fair share of hard comments, always tried to be a little supportive of the entrepreneurs coming in to the Den, especially when they were being bullied by the other Dragons!

The original panel had a real chemistry to it, filming was highly charged and great fun, and sometimes after filming all the Dragons would go on champagne fuelled jollies to one of Duncan's private member clubs or to 'The Ivy'.

I had never undertaken any 'Angel Investment' before being invited to be a Dragon, and I entered into it all with good faith and optimism, but dealing with the 'entrepreneurs' I backed on the first series proved to be something of a nightmare in itself.

My first investment was in 'Grails', the bespoke tailoring service for women. Run by ex-corporate executive Tracey Graily it was actually a brilliant concept for a business. However the logistics behind creating bespoke suits are horrifically complicated and the business was beset with operational problems. I undertook the investment in partnership with co-Dragon Doug Richard and between us we ended up injecting a total of £110,000 into the business. However, it later became apparent that much of this money was immediately evaporated to existing creditors and it didn't take Tracey long to plough her way through the entire £110k. It was our own fault of course. Firstly our due diligence should have been better, and secondly we should have retained signing control of the money, only allowing it to be spent on specific 'value-add' projects. Of course Tracey believed that the Dragons would never let her business fail, but when she came back to us asking for more money, we declined to offer any additional support. She had tried astonishingly hard to make it work, but frankly it was easier for Doug and I just to take the hit, reclaim the 60% tax rebate that comes with failed EIS investments and move on.

My second investment was in 'Le Beanock', a contemporary beanbag sofa which you hung from the rafters of your home, created by the feisty Tracie Herrtage. Having learned from my experience with Grails, this time I was careful to keep control of the cash and would only release funds to back specific 'value-add' projects. A couple of weeks after we had filmed the show I was in my car in London and saw a bus advertising the Autumn Ideal Home Show. I immediately called Tracie and said we should consider getting a last minute stand. I funded her presence at the show, as well as the creation of a really slick simple website and some promotional postcards, even though we had not yet signed contracts. There were two big learnings from being at the event (and exhibiting your product at a show is one of the best 'live' forms of market research there is). The first was that, instead of the product appealing to the cool 'urban loft dweller' as we originally thought, the ones who made a beeline for us were little kids who wanted a mini 'Le Beanock' for their bedroom. The second learning was that, at £750, Le Beanock was viewed by consumers as vastly over-priced. Given they only cost around £40 to make, I urged Tracie to lower her pricing. Unfortunately however, when we took a stand at the main Ideal Home Show the following Spring, Tracie was unable to supply the funky kid's versions in sunflower yellow and polka dots (which we had discussed we would exhibit) due to various difficulties finding fabric and problems with her workshop. By the end of the show she had made very few sales. Meanwhile Nick Rawcliffe (of Snowbone; see below), who I had also put on the stand with his hanging garden furniture, generated orders worth around £25k.

Tracie's lack of orders meant that she needed more money, but by that stage I had injected more than £50k and was not prepared to invest any more. From my dealings it was quite clear that a working relationship between us would not have worked out.

That brings us to Elizabeth Galton, the jewellery designer who I backed with Duncan. Our first revelation post show was when we looked at her financials and discovered that she had never sold anything. Nonetheless we both fell for Elizabeth's charm – Duncan clearly liked the attractive Ms Galton and I suspect that this led him to be less hard about his investment decision than he would have been otherwise.

In an attempt to gain Elizabeth some free publicity,

and because I was doing a whole day's promotional photoshoot for Red Letter Days, I agreed to be photographed naked wearing just an item of Elizabeth's jewellery. I figured that it might generate some much needed PR for Elizabeth's business. So I told Elizabeth about my idea and asked her if she had anything suitable she could lend me for the photoshoot, which would cover my modesty.

Elizabeth arrived at the photoshoot with a box inside of which was a ghastly lump of what looked like twisted copper. And although celebrity photographer Nicky Johnston, who we had hired for the shoot, did his professional best, the pics were truly awful!

Following a later discrepancy between myself and Elizabeth, I declined to continue with my planned investment in Elizabeth Galton Ltd.

I was starting to feel that many of the entrepreneurs we were offering to back on the show saw involvement by a Dragon in their business as something of a one-way gravy train.

Duncan later sold the shares he had bought for £10k to another investor for £12k (making the proud boast he had received a 20% profit on the deal).

Which finally brings us to Nick and Paddy, the 'Snowbone' boys who I backed because I could see tremendous synergies with my Red Letter Days business.

Our first exercise was to create a 'Snowbone Experience' at the Milton Keynes Snowdome, the idea being that if we could get people to trial the product they would go on to buy one. But even though the experience was priced at just £49, we only managed to muster 20 or so participants. On the day of the event I received a text from Paddy to say everything had gone fine and that it had been a brilliant day. This was followed closely by a call from one of my team supervising the event to say that a participant had cut their leg open on a Snowbone and had been rushed to hospital!

I later flew to Munich to support the boys at their first exhibition. The stand was a bit of a disaster, and despite lots of discussions about how it could be made visually exciting it featured just a plasma screen and a couple of Snowbones. Despite this being the biggest skiing and snowboarding event in the calendar, Nick and Paddy sold just one Snowbone for cash at the event, and immediately went down the pub and pissed the money up the wall. Which I guess is what you do with the money from your first sale in a business, but it did show a rather cavalier lack of respect for the fact they now had an investor on board.

After a lot of effort and input, orders for the Snowbone were simply not materialising. With the best will in the world and all the investment you can throw at it, a business without customers is always going to be doomed.

It became apparent to me quite quickly that Nick was the creative talent within the partnership and that he had used his design skills to create many brilliant and innovative products.

So I focussed my attention on mentoring and supporting him and (as I mentioned above) his presence at the Ideal Home Show really helped him on his way to generating some sales for his furniture.

Nick has since created Raw Studio and I continue to mentor and support him. He is also one of the few people I backed on the show who had the class and decency never to speak an ill word of me, which is why I continue to support him to this day, even though I have never asked for any share in his business.

Of course, all these projects, plus the literal deluge of emails I was now receiving from being on *Dragons' Den,* was a huge diversion of my energy away from running Red Letter Days.

To be honest, I was actually laying the foundations for my next business, Rachel Elnaugh Ltd, which is all about working with entrepreneurs in the small business sector, although I didn't really realise it at the time. But the whole 'Dragon' celebrity experience had actually become far more enjoyable to me than my day job at Red Letter Days, which was becoming more and more stressful.

I wasn't originally going to do the second series of *Dragons' Den,* but when the producers had problems recruiting another female Dragon they came back to me and asked if I would do it. I wasn't sure if it was the right thing, given Red Letter Days' precarious state, but I sought counsel from our then Chairman Sir Rodney Walker who thought it would be fantastic publicity and advised me to say yes and go for it.

But filming the second series was very different to filming the first. The lovely Simon Woodroffe had been replaced by the very different Theo Paphitis, who Peter had persuaded the producers to bring on to the show, and being on set was now like being in a soup of super-sized highly competitive 'Alpha Male' egos.

100 hours are filmed to create each series of approximately 5 hours of edited 'Dragon' footage, and

so the Dragons started to compete with each other to see who could give the most amusing soundbite, some of them quite nasty, to try to gain as much airtime as possible. I felt that the show was shifting away from being about trying to help budding entrepreneurs towards each Dragon trying to boost their individual fame.

The spontaneity of the show was also lost as all the entrepreneurs coming into the Den knew exactly what to expect, and either played up to the cameras (at one extreme wacky, and at the other feigning tears) in a bid to maximise their chance of not being left on the cutting room floor.

Plus more and more of the featured entrepreneurs actually declined the investment offers the Dragons made, mainly because they were all primarily there to get a free TV ad for their business.

Of all the people I offered to back, only Danny Bamping of Bedlam Puzzles accepted my offer, which I made jointly with Theo. Danny later opted not to proceed, quite frankly because he had so many advance retail orders that he didn't actually need the money.

By the third filming block in July 2005 things had reached a crisis point with Red Letter Days. A deal we had been working on fell through at the eleventh hour. I was eight months' pregnant, under extreme pressure and there was no way I could not continue to film the show. So, every evening I went straight from the set to emergency meetings in the City, face still full of TV make-up, desperately trying to corral a new deal. It was exhausting and emotionally draining. At one meeting I remember just completely breaking down in tears, black mascara running in channels down my face.

In my heart I realised that my company was slipping away from me and there was nothing that I could do to save it.

The end of Red Letter Days

I think the reality was that I had actually lost my passion for Red Letter Days, probably around early 2002. I moved from running something with great creative energy and enthusiasm to spending my days just struggling to control a big, uncontrollable machine. Despite subsequently trying to salvage the business over a ghastly and highly stressful three-year period, attempting re-financing after re-financing while I tried to bring things back into profitability, in the last week of July 2005 I knew the time had come to finally let go, and the company finally crashed into administration on 1 August 2005.

Hindsight is a wonderful thing, but looking back, there were actually three main underlying causes of the demise of Red Letter Days. Firstly, our cash flow was strangled by a credit card bond imposed on us by our bank (more on that in Chapter 7): in fact we had £3.3million cash when the bank forced us into administration.

Secondly, although all the advisors and accountants were constantly telling us we were making a profit, this never seemed to manifest itself in cash at the bank – bonded monies or otherwise. We eventually found out that the reason for this was that our call centre agents had been merrily redeeming vouchers for clients which had expired – as a result of a loophole in our software system which had been taken advantage of by an earlier customer service director, who believed that in doing so he was giving 'exceptional customer service'. Exceptional it certainly was, as his generous little commitment to customer service wiped over £3million off our bottom line. Isn't it easy to be free and easy when it's other people's money?

A total of nine different audits and independent financial reviews were done during that two-year period by various experts, but not one spotted what was going on.

By the time we fixed the issue it was far too late.

Thirdly, our operational people foolishly decided to print over £20million worth of vouchers for the retail sector, with no tracking system or security in place. That's a bit like leaving boxes of cash lying around for anyone to steal. We found a couple of boxes in a skip, a load more at one of our fulfilment houses' warehouses, and another batch were found by the police fraud squad at the home of one of our call centre staff – he had refunded over £10,000 worth to his personal credit card before a smart cookie in our accounts department noticed so many refunds to the same credit card number, and we alerted the police.

As a result, we failed every equity raising due diligence process we went into, because the contingent liabilities were perceived to be too high for any investor to take on the risk.

When the media blared that Red Letter Days had gone down with 'debts of over £10million', the reality was that the figure was much closer to £4million – the balance was made up of the notional amount that it would cost to fulfil all those retail vouchers if they ever turned up. In hindsight, the directors should only have declared actual debts on the Statement of Affairs that accompanies every administration, not all of the potential contingent liabilities. But to be honest, by that point I was past caring.

The aftermath

As it so often happens, while the business was going down my personal life was on the way up, and I married my second husband, Chris, on 2 July 2005, giving birth to my fourth son, Michael, on 25 July, just a week before the company ultimately went down.

You would think that seeing your company go into administration after a two and a half-year battle would be the end of one very long business nightmare. But the reality, as I found out the hard way, is that your nightmare has often only just begun.

I soon learned to rue the day that we chose to appoint the particular administrators of Red Letter Days, unaware that they would have a huge influence on how the case was reported to the DTI. The DTI, renamed BERR (Department for Business Enterprise & Regulatory Reform) in June 2007, investigate all companies which enter into administration, in particular how the company's affairs were run by its directors in the lead-up to its demise. If the DTI finds any 'unfit conduct', it has the power to disqualify you from becoming a director again for a minimum of two years and a maximum of 15 years. There were certainly a number of parties who, having driven the last nails into my coffin, would have loved to have seen it buried for 15 years by the DTI.

The administrators chose to base all of their findings on the limited knowledge of the only two directors remaining within the business: one an operations director (who, I suspect, had little in depth knowledge of how the refinancing of the company had been managed); the other, someone who had been on sabbatical for much of the period concerned.

Despite having been the person most closely and consistently involved in the company's financial affairs throughout the entire period, I was not consulted by the administration team once during its investigations, and therefore (unsurprisingly), when their report to the DTI was finally issued, not only was it full of inaccuracies on virtually every aspect of events leading up to the administration, it also emphatically placed all the blame on me for what had gone wrong.

Forget all you read about Gordon Brown 'wanting to make Britain more tolerant of business failure' and 'more like the USA' in its attitude to entrepreneurs who fail. The Red Letter Days crash had been extremely high profile, and as I was one of Britain's most famous entrepreneurs at the time (having just appeared on two series of BBC TV's *Dragons' Den*), I suspect the DTI would have just loved to have displayed my head on a pole in the shiny foyer of their Victoria Street offices. So much so, that, according to my lawyers, the DTI put a solicitor on the Red Letter Days case full time for 18 months, in an attempt to obtain a prosecution against me.

It's really tempting, when you receive a long letter from the DTI, asking all sorts of leading questions, to bash off an angry and indignant reply, and in fact that's exactly what I started doing. I had fought tooth and nail to save that business, and had put literally everything I had into trying to bring it back into health. To now be accused of wrong-doing really added insult to injury. But a voice inside me said: 'Rachel, don't be your normal impetuous self. Hold back and handle this properly – or you may live to regret it.'

Instead, I sent the DTI letter to a close friend and asked him for his advice. He referred me to an expert in the field, who in turn referred me to a lawyer called Ian Grier of the legal firm SGH, the top lawyers in helping directors fight DTI prosecution cases, and a guru in his field. Thankfully, although things were very financially stretched after the Red Letter Days crash, I had a significant tax repayment due to me from one of my earlier *Dragons' Den* investments where the company subsequently failed, and I just knew I had to get the best legal representation I could.

My co-directors weren't half as bothered. Despite the fact that we all received an identical letter, and that a director's disqualification applies to all the board members, none of them was particularly interested in appointing SGH to represent them – let alone meet any part of the fees – preferring instead to send in their individual (and to my mind) sketchy responses to the DTI's letter. The only contribution I received to my eventual £20,000 legal bill was a measly £400 cheque.

My husband has always laughed at me for being a bit of a hoarder, but on this occasion it was my obsession for throwing nothing away that came to my rescue. I had had the foresight to get my PA to extract 18 archive boxes of files and other paperwork from Red Letter Days' offices and deliver these to my home a few weeks before the company finally crashed. On the advice of SGH, we put together a reply to the DTI so painstakingly detailed and comprehensive that it ran to over 300 pages, containing copies of every accountant's report, insolvency advice letter, financial report and cash flow forecast that had been produced in the entire two and a half-year period. Documents that I don't think the administrators even had a clue existed.

After 18 months of investigation (and the DTI only have two years after a company has gone into administration to issue proceedings), during which the DTI held meetings with eight external parties in an attempt to uncover evidence, they dropped the case against the directors.

So brilliant were SGH at fighting my corner that I now wish I had appointed them to advise me way before Red Letter Days crashed. With hindsight, I know that with Ian and his team's help I could almost certainly have found a solution to the company's problems. But entrepreneurs are optimistic creatures and I always felt, practically right up to the very last minute on the day we went into administration, that a solution would be found. In business there is often an incredibly fine line between success and failure.

So I started out at the age of 24 with nothing and 16 years later ended up with virtually nothing (in purely monetary terms) except the experience of the most incredible rollercoaster ride that is 'being an entrepreneur'.

Although, to be fair, I had also acquired a certain 'celebrity entrepreneur' status via my appearance on the first two series of *Dragons' Den*, which was already starting to generate me substantials fees for speaking events and endorsement deals – along with a fair degree of the kind of personal wealth that comes from earning a good salary and a few good dividend payouts over a number of years.

When my business folded, many people sent me their condolences, as if the loss of Red Letter Days was the most terrible thing that could ever have happened to me, akin to the death of a loved one. When I was fighting to save the business that was how I saw 'failure' too. But other, more enlightened, observers simply said to me, 'Rachel, you'll look back on this period in years to come and realise that this is probably the best thing that ever happened to you.'

I now realise that, similar to my time at Andersen's 20 years earlier, there comes a time to let go in order to allow new opportunities to flow into your life. In some respect, we are constantly being given the training and opportunities that will equip us for the next stage in our life. It is all part of the process that allows us to grow.

Those final two and a half years before the crash of Red Letter Days were horrible and were indeed my personal business nightmare. I discuss much of what happened to me during this time throughout the chapters in this book, relating it to the experiences of others – proving that, however bad it gets, someone has always been there before you. Suffice it to say, I learned more in those last years of Red Letter Days about business than I learned in the entire previous decade. But I would not wish the experience on anyone.

I will end my story with my favourite inspirational piece by Theodore Roosevelt, which I think perfectly sums up my own entrepreneurial journey:

> *It is not the critic who counts: nor the man who points out how the strong man stumbles, or where the doer of deeds could have done better. The credit belongs to the man who is actually in the arena, whose face is marred by dust and sweat and blood, who strives valiantly, who errs and comes up short again and again, because there is no effort without error or shortcoming, but who knows the great enthusiasms, the great devotions, who spends himself for a worthy cause; who, at the best, knows, in the end, the triumph of high achievement, and who, at the worst, if he fails, at least he fails while daring greatly, so that his place shall never be with those cold and timid souls who know neither victory nor defeat.*

1

THE OVEREXPANSION TRAP

By far the most people-orientated Dragon of them all was Simon Woodroffe OBE, founder of the innovative restaurant chain Yo! Sushi, whom I had the pleasure of working with in the first series of *Dragons' Den*. He was always the most supportive of the entrepreneurs coming on the show, and if any of them got into difficulties he would go to their assistance rather than let them squirm in front of the cameras. All that was edited out of the final show of course – and I suspect his 'niceness' was the reason he left after only one series.

Simon was a late starter in business. While he was growing up, his father was an army officer and so he had a fairly stuffy upbringing. By way of rebellion he left school at 16 with just two O Levels and started out as a roadie in the rock 'n' roll business.

'Going on tour with bands like Jethro Tull, The Faces and the Moody Blues were incredible highs. It was my dream to hang out with those people. Then becoming a stage designer took me into a different echelon. But obviously there were also lots of lows which came crashing in, including the collapse of my marriage after just one and a half years. But the biggest high I ever had was setting up Yo! Sushi.'

Simon was 45 when he founded the brilliant concept for a restaurant chain in 1997, after a visit to Japan where a Japanese friend suggested that he should create a conveyor-belt sushi restaurant in London. He had no experience in the restaurant industry, but his background in entertainment gave him the perfect experience to create a restaurant that was pure theatre.

It took Simon two years to get Yo! Sushi from an idea to a reality. He put in all his savings, as well as money from friends and family. 'When I look back I'm not quite sure how I pulled it off. It was incredibly high risk – it was a restaurant after all – but I knew I was doing it right.

'I really enjoyed the creative process of putting the whole thing together and also during those two years I was never being judged by anybody because it hadn't opened. I always say business is like life: it's very messy, and if you can keep a sense of direction while everyone is losing their head and blaming it on you, it will all come together at some stage later on. Most people can't cope with that messiness because they like their lives to be ordered, and that's what leads many people to fail in business, because they can't see their way through the problems.

'When it actually came to opening the first Yo! Sushi restaurant, it was an incredibly stressful few weeks and then everything just seemed to come right. We were

With my brothers (left to right) Mark, John and Luke, 1969

Skiing in France in early 1989, aged 24. I created Red Letter Days in July of that year.

With my friend the writer Scott McRae, who came up with the name 'Red Letter Days', on a cruise around Boston Harbour, c.1996

At the Indian ceremony to celebrate my engagement to my first husband Lax Kabra, early 1990

My husband Chris and I at our wedding celebration at Sharrow Bay Hotel, Lake District, 2 July 2005

Christmas 2007, in Bakewell with my husband Chris and our five sons (left to right) Mark, Paul, Eddie, Michael and baby Jack

At our first corporate show, 'Incentive 94'

With 'Mr Motivator' and members of the Red Letter Days team, at the David Lloyd club in North Finchley, 1995

Finalists of the Veuve Clicquot Business Woman of the Year Award 2001. From left to right: Chey Garland, Sly Bailey, Jo Malone and Barbara Cassani (who won). 'Always the bridesmaid...!'

With Linda Bennett (LK Bennett) and other winners of Ernst & Young Entrepreneur of the Year Award, June 2002

Meeting HRH Prince Charles at St James' Palace, autumn 2002

In 'dominatrix mode' – a picture taken for fun as part of a larger photo shoot, December 2004

The 'Mystery Experience Night' I organised for my marketing team to celebrate my 37th birthday, 11 December 2001. In a super-stretch limo on the way to an upmarket bar crawl of London – with (left to right) Simon, Jacqueline, Murray and Gwen...

...and later in the Purple Bar at Sanderson with (left to right) Jacqueline, Gwen, Sarah and Murray

The brilliant James Dyson

The re-born Gerald Ratner

A young Dawn Gibbins

The very classy Nick Wheeler

In bed with Simon Woodroffe at YOTEL!

Young upstart James Murray Wells

The Dragon line up after Series Two: (left to right) myself, Duncan Bannatyne, Doug Richard, Theo Paphitis and Peter Jones

The charismatic Jeffrey Archer in his stunning London penthouse apartment

Super-celeb Peter Jones

The wonderful Doug Richard

The original Dragons (left to right) Peter Jones, Doug Richard, myself, Duncan Bannatyne and Simon Woodroffe

taking a lot of money. It was just like having a hit record. But even then it didn't feel secure – not for three or four years. I always thought it was like a pack of cards, and a fairly precarious pack of cards at that. Every new site that we opened could easily have gone wrong.'

The mistake that entrepreneurs often make in business is to think that the initial success they have had with their first project can easily be replicated. However, in business – and particularly in retail and leisure – there is often a very magical mix of ingredients which has to be just right to create the conditions for success. Get any ingredient wrong in the roll-out process and it is very easy for your expansion to fail.

The first Yo! Sushi restaurant was in London's Soho – busy and bustling with tourist trade all day long. Create a similar restaurant in a business area and it's easy to be busy every lunchtime, but that narrow window of peak trading often isn't enough to create the kind of returns that are needed to make your investment pay.

It was not long before the ambitious expansion of the Yo! restaurant chain started to run into serious problems, as it was not generating enough cash to fund the growth, and the business desperately needed an injection of cash.

When you are in business and find yourself in that situation, and where your bank has an exposure to risk, you often find your account transferred to the 'special recovery unit' – a sort of financial intensive care unit where some very unforgiving and hard banking people watch you like hawks until you have resolved your problems, usually through an external investment from a venture capitalist, and until the bank is in the clear.

I went through this experience with Red Letter Days at about the same time Simon was going through his. We both banked with the same bank and both shared the same special recovery bank manager.

When you run a successful business and are first lured into becoming a corporate banking client, you are treated like the Queen – lavish meetings in wonderfully furnished meeting rooms with plenty of fresh coffee served in china and plates of delicious biscuits.

By contrast, a bank's special recovery unit is often a shabby set of offices with fraying carpets and plastic furniture, where you are treated like a naughty schoolgirl who has arrived to be punished, and are lucky if you are offered a vending-machine coffee in a polystyrene cup.

So the Venture Capital process begins – an agonising round of presentations (think *Dragons' Den*, except a hundred times more humiliating when the money you need is not just for expansion but to get yourself out of a hole you have already created), to unsympathetic City types whose only thought is how much money they are likely to make out of you as a result of the deal.

Hopefully, as a result of the process you will receive a number of offers and then you will usually be obliged to enter into 'exclusivity' with them – meaning that you put all the other offers on hold while the VC of your choice does their due diligence process (essentially looking at all the financial, legal and commercial aspects of your business) and hopefully completes on the deal.

More likely however, is that the VC will latch on to some weakness in the business which they have discovered while looking at your books and renege on the original deal in some way, either by pulling out altogether or by changing the terms to take more equity. This usually happens at the last minute, by which point you will typically be three months into the negotiations, and when time is running out, particularly if you are undertaking a refinance for cash flow reasons. The VC will know this and will not hesitate to take advantage of their power in that situation.

In the same way, Simon and his team set about to resolving his business crisis. At first they tried to get investment from 3i (the largest venture capitalist organisation in the country) but the deal soon collapsed. They then went back to Primary Capital, who had originally made them an offer, but due to the failed deal with 3i, Primary immediately reduced the terms of their original offer.

'To be honest I didn't blame them. I had never done a VC deal before and these guys are fairly aggressive. But fair enough, what do they know about business, what creative thing have they ever done? Making money out of investments is the world that they are in.

'Robin Roland, my partner in the business by this time, led the cavalry charge to get the deal done, much more so than I. It was quite a good partnership because I just sat there acting like the one who needed to be persuaded to complete.

'Actually it was quite cheeky, as we were in a precarious situation financially; we were running out of money and the estate by this point was fairly run down and needed a lot of repairs doing. I knew in my heart of hearts that the VC deal could easily have gone wrong. But later on, after we completed, the VC always said they thought I would be the one to pull out, not them. So I think maybe playing that double act was the thing that clinched it for us.'

Simon was also quite clever in the way he structured the deal. While the overexpansion of Yo! Sushi essentially lost him his controlling stake in the business, he negotiated a multi-million-pound lump-sum pay-off, as well as retaining a minority shareholding in the refinanced business, plus the rights to roll out the Yo! brand into other sectors.

'So of course you turn up to the meeting to sign the contracts and they said to me "Where do you want the money?" To be honest I hadn't really thought about creating a special account for it so I just had it credited to my current account. Then they cracked open the champagne to celebrate the completion of the deal and all these horrible lawyers suddenly turned into nice people with a proper sense of humour.

'I went back home a bit tipsy and on the corner near my home there was a cash machine, and I couldn't resist going to check my balance. When I put in my card, up came all these zeros; for the first time in my life I had a few million quid and it was all mine. There was a bloke standing behind me waiting to use the machine and I turned and said to him "Cop a look at this mate!" I think I still have that balance print-out somewhere to remind me of that day.

'If anyone tells you money doesn't make you happy, they are lying.'

Simon has since launched a number of Yo! ventures but the biggest project yet is YOTEL – the Japanese-style capsule hotel, designed for transit stays and stopovers where all you need is a bed for the night.

'I was lucky enough to get an upgrade to the sleeper bed in British Airways first class. I went to sleep with the conundrum of how to make a Japanese capsule hotel acceptable in the West and woke up realising the solution was around me: all I needed to do was find the designer of the BA first class cabin and ask them to help me design a hotel.'

The first YOTEL opened in Gatwick in 2007, followed by Heathrow and Amsterdam's Schiphol airport in early 2008. Simon has learned from his earlier mistakes and obtained substantial funding for the business at the outset, in the form of private backing from a Kuwaiti family.

'My life has been driven by the fear of financial insecurity and money has been really important to me. However, time is my most valuable commodity now. It's like there's only so much time left.

'I have realised at 55 that it's OK for things to be just OK – I don't have to be on the biggest TV show or to have the biggest thing; for me being OK is enough. I've now got partners for everything I do and I am almost at the point now where I have freedom from all the anxiety that I have had in business over the years – anxiety of losing everything, getting things wrong, business relationships going wrong, suppliers not turning up – all the nightmares that you have with a business. I think you've got to go through the highs and lows of business at some time in your life, but for me I have come out of that, and now just being OK is good enough.'

It has since been announced that Yo! Sushi has been sold for £51million. Brilliant news for Simon, whose 22% stake will have netted him around £10million. He even managed to retain a worldwide royalty in perpetuity so that he gets a percentage of every penny spent in the restaurants forever. Frankly, more than just an 'OK' deal, and no one deserves it more.

So it turns out, as is so often the case, that Simon's business nightmare actually led to wealth beyond his wildest dreams, as well as the most valuable commodity of the all – freedom. I think that sometimes in business, success is just a case of being able to hold your nerve.

Looking back, I wish I had been as smart as Simon when I went through my Red Letter Days recovery years. We too went through the whole charade of the VC process, we were offered several really good deals, and the one that I opted for was from a team of people whom I felt I could really trust and work with (unlike Simon, the plan was that I would remain in the business).

However, when they reneged at the 11th hour and demanded a 51% controlling stake in the business rather than the 33% we had originally agreed, my instinct was that I could not work with such people. Despite being told by everyone at the time (in particular my finance director, who stood to take 5% of the company) that I had no alternative but to take the deal, I broke loose, took a second opinion, and brought in external assistance which allowed us to release £3million cash into the business within just six weeks. But the bank made sure that the naughty schoolgirl who managed to wriggle off their hook would be taught a lesson – and the rest, as they say, is business history.

Looking back, I can't think of a worse existence than the stress of running a business which you need to microwave for profit (i.e. accelerate short-term returns at the expense of your brand or longer-term growth) to satisfy your VC investor, and I now realise that going down that route would probably have proved to be a living hell for me. If I had been smarter, I would have negotiated a deal which delivered me a lump sum, like Simon, and agreed to step back from the business, but sometimes (and particularly as a woman) you just get too emotionally attached to your baby to see the logical solution.

These are my thoughts on how to grow your business while avoiding over-expanding:

- Just because you have created a successful business in one location, don't assume your formula will work everywhere.
- Conducting market research to ensure you have the right customer mix is key before opening branches in any other location.
- Make sure you have the right operational platform in terms of systems, management information and administrative support to create a firm foundation for the new larger business. You will need to be able to control what is going on.
- If you need to expand to reach another level in your business, find the finance BEFORE you embark on the project. It's much easier to negotiate good terms when your business is in the ascendancy, than when you are trying to dig yourself out of a hole.
- Consider franchising as an alternative option to expand the business. It de-risks things for you as well as providing your business an additional revenue stream. Franchising has enabled great businesses like McDonald's and The Body Shop to become worldwide brands within a very short space of time.
- Be mindful that many entrepreneurs have gone down the VC route and lived to regret it. Perhaps you should consider growing your business organically – it's far less risky, less stressful, and you will remain in control of your future.

2

THE DEVIL IS IN THE DETAIL

The problem with being your own boss is that you don't have anyone to answer to (except maybe your publisher!) so it's very easy – especially if you work from home – to get a bit lazy and opt out of doing any work if the mood takes you. This is why I always advocate building a business based on something you love, because that way work is pure enjoyment – something that you eagerly look forward to each day, rather than being a chore you resent.

So, much as I was looking forward to interviewing Channel 4's *Make Me A Million* star Ivan Massow, there was a huge temptation to cancel our meeting in favour of a day at home enjoying the spring sunshine in our beautiful garden overlooking the Peak District. Then self-discipline kicked in. It had taken a long time to find a date in both our diaries, as Ivan is rarely in the UK, and so I found myself getting into my hot car for the five-hour round trip to Bristol.

I am so glad that I did, as (unknown to me), it was the eve of Ivan's court appearance in the case that Zurich Insurance had launched against him. If they won, Ivan would be made bankrupt. Unwilling to pay the lawyer's fees to fight such a corporate giant, Ivan had chosen to defend himself.

Thus, our meeting at an Italian restaurant in Bristol opened with Ivan telling me he planned to spend our lunch together getting drunk on Pinot Grigio – an option that was alas not open to me, not just because of my long drive home, but also because I was four months pregnant at the time.

By way of background to all this, Ivan started his working life in the insurance industry in the 1980s and had the idea to create his own insurance business specialising in meeting the needs of homosexual men. This was at a time when AIDs had just broke on the scene; homophobia was rife and gay men found it extremely difficult to buy life assurance from the mainstream insurance companies.

So in 1990 Massow Financial Services was born, run on a shoestring budget from a squat in London. Despite the fact that the insurance sector was saturated at the time, Ivan quickly found that he had hit upon a niche market.

The fact that Ivan was highly critical of the insurance industry, and Allied Dunbar in particular, attracted a huge amount of publicity, and led to Ivan becoming something of an icon for gay men's rights. 'Allied Dunbar had just run an advertising campaign with the strapline "For The Life You May Not Know". So I plastered Soho with posters from my business aimed at the gay market entitled "For The Life You May Not Want Allied Dunbar To Know",' Ivan told me.

The cheeky campaign worked, and Ivan's business grew rapidly. By 1997, Massow Financial Services was the 10th largest independent financial adviser in the UK and was valued at £22million.

Ivan later sold the company to Rainbow Finance, which sadly then crashed spectacularly. He returned to help his old team form Ivan Massow Consultants from the ashes.

Meanwhile Zurich, one of the world's largest insurance companies, had bought Allied Dunbar. It seems they had been observing Ivan's success from afar. Some years later, Ivan met with one of their directors, who had been around during the rather embarrassing ad campaign.

'He told me that the company's view on the gay market had changed completely and offered to bring my business under the wing of Zurich as one of their franchisees, as part of which they would refinance the business and help us grow our service offer together' recounts Ivan.

'He told me that they would supply the offices and the back office support, and for my part I would supply my brand and our client base and be the figurehead of the business. It took six months to negotiate the terms of the deal, at the end of which I received a pre-printed contract full of boring detail, and I just signed it.'

Like many entrepreneurs, attention to detail – in particular ploughing through pages of tightly written legal wording – was anathema to Ivan, and crucially he didn't invest in a good lawyer to go through everything with a fine toothcomb.

'One of the clauses, hiding away in three folders of paperwork which were 12 inches thick, stated that nothing discussed and no documentation exchanged prior to the signing of the contract was relevant to the deal.' This is called an 'entire agreement' clause, meaning all promises and assurances made about how a business would be run post-deal are irrelevant unless they are specifically stated in the contract. These clauses are quite standard, but many entrepreneurs won't know that.

Ivan continues: 'One of my requirements for the office space – which I saw and agreed prior to signing – was that we would have a proper space with its own entrance with lifts and wheelchair access, firstly because we needed to preserve our clients' confidentiality and secondly because some were ill and in wheelchairs. After we had signed the contract and the deal completed, we were given a space at the back of a very large open-plan office and expected to hot desk with other staff.

'But one of the biggest issues was that they wouldn't allow two men to apply for insurance together, which causes a huge problem if you are trying to buy life assurance cover for a property purchase which will pay out on the first death of either party.

'There's a part of me that feels that this was retribution for the campaign I had run against them. We're talking about middle managers with small pockets of power – power that can destroy you if exercised in the wrong way.'

Ivan saw his oversight of the entire agreement clause as a betrayal by Zurich, and he now feels really let down: 'It's a bit like me agreeing to sell you an Audi and giving you a contract where hidden on page 73 is a clause saying "If an Audi isn't available we will deliver you a rusty 1960s mini instead" and if you miss that clause – perhaps because you are having a glass of wine at the time – it's completely your fault.'

So Ivan pulled out of the franchise arrangement and continued operating as an independent business again. But his business as an independent failed this time, which Ivan believes was because his reputation within the gay market was destroyed by his time with Zurich. Rightly or wrongly, Ivan believes that his ad campaign in the 1990s was at the root of the problem and that this was retribution.

As part of the franchise deal, Zurich made an advance to the company of £330,000 to cover relocation costs – and Ivan had personally guaranteed this. Ivan pulled out of the franchise agreement and so his business collapsed. Zurich then tried to call in his personal guarantee. If he had paid he would have been bankrupt and so he didn't. Zurich then issued court proceedings, and Ivan fought back with a counterclaim for £13million damages arising from the failure of his business, which he said was a result of inappropriate actions by Zurich.

I am having lunch with Ivan the day before the hearing. The great thing about Ivan is that he is hugely charismatic, terribly charming and also incredibly attractive. So, as he downs the Pinot Grigio and we eat our avocado and seafood starter, Ivan becomes increasingly entertaining company. This is a man who is about to face the death sentence tomorrow, but he's intent on going out smiling.

The irony of the whole situation is that Ivan really isn't hung up on material wealth at all. He lives in a rented apartment in Barcelona and, like all sensible wealth creators who are facing financial ruin, he's already given everything away – leaving only an old camper van and a dog for Zurich to re-possess should they win the following day, but plenty of friends willing to help should he need to lay his hands on cash.

For Ivan is a man who, even if penniless, could live like a king – simply because of his divine charm and personality. So our lunch extends until mid-afternoon, by which time the restaurant is empty, as are the bottles of Pinot Grigio.

Before I finally leave Ivan, I end our interview by giving him my speciality 'Rachel pep talk': that he should fight to the death and use his fame to help his cause; to be the David that beats their Goliath – rather than just drowning in a sea of wine.

Two days later I opened my email to a plethora of Ivanrelated Google Alerts. He managed to get himself an interview with Jon Snow on *Channel 4 News*, the press picked up on the story and most of the TV and radio stations had him on their shows the next morning. The judge had given Ivan the chance to take his case to a full trial.

However his victory and the PR field day were short-lived. The judge had said that if Ivan wanted to take his case to trial then he would need to pay money into court. Ivan didn't do this and so two weeks later Zurich was granted summary judgement – and Ivan was ordered to pay the whole of the debt as well as legal costs.

On reflection, although Zurich won the legal claim I suspect that this has still cost them dearly.

So do yourself a favour: always read the small print.

A few observations on major contracts and handling litigation:

- Get the best legal advice money can buy, even if you can't afford it. Believe it or not, there are some people who actually enjoy reviewing legal documentation!
- Don't just check what's in the contract: look for what has been omitted. This is especially so if the legal documentation has been drawn up by the other party – it will always reflect their own most important criteria, not yours.
- Think of all the things that could possibly go wrong with the deal. How are your interests protected?
- No matter what assurances you may receive, and no matter how pleasant the other party appears to be, this is business. Trust no one.

3

REPLACING YOURSELF CAN PROVE EXPENSIVE

Of all the people whom I interviewed to write this book, I don't think there was one I identified with more than Nick Wheeler, the creator of the Charles Tyrwhitt mail-order shirts brand.

I first met Nick when we were both speaking at the Growing Business Live conference. Luckily he went on stage after me – he did a brilliantly entertaining presentation about how he had built the Charles Tyrwhitt brand, which put all the other speakers that day in the shade.

Nick is an entrepreneur who has built his mail-order company from scratch; he has been stitched up (forgive the pun) on more than one occasion, but has survived through it and taken his business to a turnover of £50 million.

He's also, famously, married to Chrissie Rucker (founder of The White Company) whom I also interviewed for this book, but, rather irritatingly, it seems she's never really put a business foot wrong! Like the golden Head Girl at school who is always impeccably behaved, and then sails in with 'A' grades in all her exams. This would explain why this year Chrissie's turnover will eclipse her husband's for the first time, despite the fact that he has been in business longer.

I expected Nick's head office to be based above a posh shop in Jermyn Street (Essex girl as I am, I pronounced it as 'Germaine' and was quickly corrected by Nick that it was 'German'). Instead, I arrived for my interview at a scruffy industrial unit on the bleak business estate opposite the BBC in White City.

Nick is very Sloane, but likeable with it; he clearly knows his target customer inside out but is equally a grafter and definitely not a snob. Charles Tyrwhitt is, in fact, a very down-to-earth business.

There were lots of things we discussed in our interview that could have made it into this book, but Nick's biggest business crisis was his decision to step back from running the business and hand over the reins to a 'proper' MD.

In fact, during our interview he reminded me of the words I had said to him a year or so earlier at Growing Business Live, after he mentioned to me that he'd just brought in a managing director to 'run things', to which I replied 'Are you sure you're doing the right thing? That's exactly the mistake I made and it's what brought my business down.'

It turns out that Nick chose the wrong person to place at the helm of his ship – and paid the price for it 18 months later.

Like me, Nick had started his mail-order business from scratch, although his first sale was in 1986 and mine was in 1989. He built Charles Tyrwhitt Shirts on a shoestring budget, testing and trialling and slowly building turnover until he worked out a formula that worked. Simply through giving great quality and service, he built his mail-order database to the point where, together with expansion into nine retail shops, he was turning over £40million.

Then (like me in 2002) he had a crisis of confidence.

'If you start something young, where you don't have any other experience, you just feel your way the whole time, just using your common sense. By September 2005 we had a £40million turnover and I felt we needed to take it to £100million. I just felt I wasn't the right person to take it from 40 to 100, I thought I needed someone with much more bigger company experience.

'I started to compare myself to Michael Dell; he is the same age as me, he started his business (Dell Computers) at the same time, in fact everything was the same – except that he now has a $60billion turnover business!

'It's interesting in our little world of mail order that there are very few businesses which have broken through the £50million barrier. Boden are doing bloody well. They did £120million-plus last year; they have got it right and they are really on a roll. I like Johnny [Boden], but I feel rather narked – in the nicest possible way – that he has done so well.

'So you just get to a certain stage in the growth of the business and think "Am I the right person?" and just feel a complete idiot because you've got there by using your common sense, whereas all these other bright guys have been to Harvard Business School.'

Nick approached a head-hunter to find him the high-calibre MD he was after; she recommended someone straightaway. 'I met him and I just thought he was damned good. I am a very instinctive judge of people and I tend to make snap decisions. To be honest, it's probably much better to sleep on decisions. I realised at the time that this was a very big decision for me – this was the guy who was either going to cock things up or he was going to take it to £100million and beyond – nothing in between.'

This new MD was involved for about 18 months, giving Nick the opportunity to step back and 'oversee' the business. 'It's difficult because if you bring in an MD to run the business, then you cannot interfere the whole time, you have to give them space. If you give them space, of course you run the risk that they will cock things up. But if you don't give them space then it's not going to work, every time.

'With hindsight you can look back and see the mistakes you made. This guy had been at Ralph Lauren for 15 years. Ralph Lauren is a very big and successful business, but he wasn't MD – he didn't actually run Ralph Lauren – he was a senior vice president, responsible for sales and marketing in Europe. He was used to having that massive support structure around him and I would never, if I was appointing an MD again, appoint someone who did not actually have MD experience. That is fundamental, you've got to have run a business and you've also got to have run a similar-sized business. You don't want someone who has run a business with just five people, but equally you don't want someone who has run a massive corporation with all the back-up and support.

'He came into the business and was so passionate about it; in fact he almost loved the business as much as I do. The problem was, he came from Ralph Lauren and he wanted to make us into Ralph Lauren and I went along with it. So if there is blame to be had it lies mainly on my shoulders. I thought it would broaden the product range, but I had been in the business 20 years and should have known and understood what made us tick.

'The problem with mail order is that it has a very long lead time, it's like a super tanker because you're working on products a year in advance, so it takes time to discover that things aren't working out. So the fact that it did not work out has just put us back two years.

'In business you run into this problem that there is a circle of MDs who just move from the business to the next. They move on and you're not going to give them a bad reference; you don't want them to take you to tribunal, you just want to end it amicably, so you tell people they were 'fine' and off they go to another job.

'We are still friends. He is a great guy and very talented. Just not right for Charles Tyrwhitt. I am certainly not vindictive in any way, we haven't argued and I hope we will be good friends. But it is quite fun to be back in the business running things, and in that respect again I am quite like Michael Dell, who has also had to go back into it, which is quite funny. I'm a great believer in the future, so I always think things will get better as time goes on.'

Nick survived his sabbatical as MD and his business, although set back in its expansion plans, still lived to tell the tale. I was of course less lucky, and although it only took me nine months to discover that things were going badly wrong, enough damage was done during that time to ultimately bring my business down.

Like Nick, I had made the mistake of recruiting my MD from a big company, where he had had huge budgets to play with and the umbrella of a large organisation to cushion the business from any mistakes. The worst that can happen to a big company MD if they fail is that they lose their job (usually with a huge severance payout to cushion the blow), so there's really very little downside to being gung-ho.

An entrepreneur, on the other hand, has a great deal more to lose. They've usually invested their entire savings, as well as many years of their life, into building their business. While entrepreneurs are natural risk takers, most of the moves they make are still calculated, and based on knowing the business inside out. But most importantly of all, they have usually built everything on a shoestring and know how hard it is to make money – so they hate spending a penny more than is absolutely necessary. The big company MD, conversely, loves nothing more than ploughing his way through other people's money. After all it's much easier (and much more fun) to spend it than it is to make it.

This makes the odds of an externally recruited MD coming in and transforming your business from a £50million company to a £100million one extremely low. After all, if they did have that skill, why on earth would they be working for you and not running their own show?

Many people believe entrepreneurs are only good for the first stages of the business journey; yet I have heard so many horror stories of MDs not working out that I think stepping aside is one of the most disastrous risks an entrepreneur can take with their business. Even those publicly quoted companies with huge budgets to play with and which have outgrown their founders (think easyJet, The Body Shop and Laura Ashley) quickly lose the original magic of their brand and eventually become a cash machine with limited shelf life that has to be milked for profit as quickly as it can.

In my view, as long as an entrepreneur still has their passion for the business they created they will always have more value to add.

If I had to give my five top tips on how to avert disaster when handing over the reins of your business they would be:

- Groom someone from within the business to be your successor and work with them for several years, slowly giving them more and more authority until eventually they are doing your job.
- If you must recruit from the outside, ensure that your new MD has to make a substantial investment in the business, so that if it doesn't work out, the appointment will hurt them as much as it hurts you – avoid 'upside-only' packages with long notice periods and share option packages.
- Ensure that you have a rock-solid finance director whom you can trust to control expenditure.
- Make sure that you are receiving thorough and accurate management information throughout the entire process.
- Better still, do the handover as part of a refinancing deal where you sell part of your stake to a third party (eg a venture capitalist) so that you have a chunk of cash ready in case it all goes badly wrong, but a share in the business should everything come up roses.

4

DON'T LOSE CONTROL OF THE CASH

Writing a book is everyone's dream and so I consider myself lucky to have actually been asked to do this one, but as Jeffrey Archer (see Chapter 6) warned me, actually executing the task takes huge self-discipline and stamina.

I also made the mistake of thinking that TIME would be the key resource I needed to complete my masterpiece, and therefore gave myself plenty. I was determined to take three months out of my diary to devote to maternity leave this time around, so I reasoned that this would give me the perfect opportunity to work through all the research and interviews I had done in the previous six months and to complete the finished manuscript in time for my deadline.

But I was wrong.

It is not time that you need to write a book, it is INSPIRATION – which doesn't always flow when all your hormones are focused on nesting and motherhood, rather than business insight and wisdom.

So, much to the annoyance of my publisher, I was forced to negotiate an extension, and thus it was something of a relief when I finally got back on the business circuit after the birth of my son.

I desperately needed re-energising, and despite my deep-seated fear of public speaking, going back to appearing at business events was the way that I achieved it.

There was a time during my Red Letter Days years when I used to just swoop in, speak at an event, and then fly back out again. I was far too busy to invest any more time than I had to in anything other than running my business. But luckily my passion these days is about inspiring, motivating and helping others achieve business success – which you can't readily do unless you feel inspired yourself. So, although I am still on 'output' for much of my time, I also have the luxury of spending at least part of every week on 'input': networking, researching, reading and attending events. Thankfully, minus the guilt that normally goes with it.

Recently I was lucky enough to be appearing atan event in Newcastle where the award-winning entrepreneur Michelle Mone (head of MJM International and creator of the Ultimo bra) was also speaking about her entrepreneurial journey.

I'd met Michelle a few years before – at a networking event for high-profile female entrepreneurs (in the days when I used to get invites to such events; that is, before Red Letter Days crashed and I found myself mysteriously deleted from all the invitation lists!). To be honest, I'd always felt a bit jealous of Michelle (and I do think there is generally a huge amount of rivalry between female entrepreneurs). She's tall, blonde and attractive, and has of course had huge success with her revolutionary gel-filled bras. But I now realise just how many business nightmares Michelle has lived through on her journey to becoming the huge entrepreneurial success story she now is.

Brought up in the poor parts of Glasgow without even a bath in the house, her father chronically ill, her mother suffering from depression and her 10-month-old brother dying in hospital of spina bifida without her ever being allowed to see him, Michelle could easily have figured that life really didn't hold much promise for her. But those early hardships simply served to forge Michelle's sense of determination – one of the key qualities of the successful entrepreneur.

After several entrepreneurial enterprises, and during a night out in 1996, Michelle was inspired to create the Ultimo bra; the idea came while she was complaining to her husband how uncomfortable her Wonderbra was. Borrowing the idea of silicone gel implants from the cosmetic surgery industry, she created a super-comfy new style of push-up bra into which she ploughed all of her savings.

She managed to persuade Selfridges to stock the bra for its launch in 1999, and having no money left for a grand advertising campaign, she decided to use PR to the max: she paid some actors £500 to pose as cosmetic surgeons staging a protest in London's Oxford Street to ban the Ultimo bra on the basis that it would put them out of business. That simple stunt led to huge amounts of free publicity for the bra. So much so that Selfridges' initial three months' stock sold out within the first week – turning the 'Ultimo' into a retail phenomenon.

Along with orders from UK stores, word soon spread internationally and it wasn't long before SAKS Fifth Avenue were on the phone placing orders too. But the real PR coup was the money-can't-buy marketing that resulted when Julia Roberts wore an 'Ultimo' in the Oscar-winning film *Erin Brockovich* (2000).

Now riding high on the roller coaster of expansion (which so frequently happens once a business takes off – you are so busy that you don't always take time to stop and think), Michelle appointed distributors in both the USA and Australia to quickly get her product into the retail sector. The Ultimo bra was going down a storm.

But overnight, disaster struck when her distributors disappeared with all her stock, along with £600,000 in cash receipts for orders taken. This goes to show how quickly a brilliant business can unravel through one simple mistake or error of judgement. As with many entrepreneurs before her, support from Michelle's bank quickly evaporated at this first sign of trouble – despite the fact that she had just negotiated a £15million contract with leading department store Debenhams.

Facing voluntary liquidation, Michelle desperately needed a financial lifeline. This is where Michelle's rock-solid determination and gritted tenacity made all the difference between success and failure.

At about that time, quite through chance, Michelle found herself sitting next to an engaging man at a business event. She asked for his business card and discovered that he was European head of one of the world's largest banks. The next day she called him to ask if the bank would intervene and rebank her to help save the business.

Time was not on her side, and the wheels of the banking industry typically move very slowly. But in this instance the bank pulled out the stops, which meant the business was able to honour the Debenhams contract, and the company's financial fortunes very quickly turned around.

Famously, Michelle went on to replace the original 'face' of the Ultimo brand, Rod Stewart's wife Penny Lancaster, with his ex-wife Rachel Hunter – generating millions of pounds' worth more of free publicity. She has now built the business to a level where it is worth in the region of £60million.

As I listened to Michelle tell her story – and engage the entire audience with her infectious enthusiasm and self-deprecating sense of humour – it was easy to see how she won so much support during her hour of need. For Michelle is a fighter, and financial backers love fighters. Any fool can run a business while it is riding high; it's in the desperate hours of need that an entrepreneur's true colours show through.

As I listened and laughed, and admired all of Michelle's brilliant triumphs over adversity, it was difficult not to sit there and wonder whether I could have done things differently and survived my own patch of adversity with my business Red Letter Days. Maybe if I had had better connections in the banking sector or, even just the extra energy to fight on for a few hours more, things would have had a very different outcome.

Undoubtedly the strongest message that I gleaned from listening to Michelle was that you have to move forward in life, playing whatever hand you are dealt, rather than wasting energy immersed in bitterness and regret.

Michelle's business nightmare resulted from misplaced trust, allowing third parties to control part of the business's money. Whoever holds the money also holds the power to destroy a business, should they decide not to release it back to you, whether that is an overseas distributor, or even a fellow director who has signing authority to the company's money, or, as in Red Letter Days' case, our bank, whose credit card bond forced the company into administration, despite the business having £3.3million cash at the bank.

So, whatever else you may decide to delegate, keep your cash close and under your direct control, for it is always cash (or rather, lack of it) that will force you out of business every time.

Six insights on keeping control of the cash:

- Ensure that you have counter-signing authority on all payments out of the business. Signing authority is the last thing you should delegate.
- Watch purchase-order authority levels and don't allow anyone other than yourself to sign major contracts or even commit the business to anything, whether verbally or in writing.
- In any joint venture, ensure that the cash flows into your account, not your partner's.
- Don't offer credit, or advances of money or stock, to anyone if you can help it. Even blue-chip companies can hold you to ransom in this way.
- If you find yourself having problems with your bank or if your credit card provider is 'bonding' your cash, either change banks or route payments via an overseas subsidiary.
- In business, 'cash is king'. Make sure you know on a daily basis exactly how much money there is in the bank – and how long it will last you. This is one area of the business that you cannot and must not delegate.

5

TAKE CASH NOT PAPER

The moment your business begins making waves in the market you will start to be approached by people who want to buy you. This is of course very flattering, and the temptation is to start thinking about selling out.

Unfortunately this can be a very dangerous change of mindset, because you subtly move from being 100% focused on running a great business for the long term, to becoming 100% focused on finding your ultimate exit. This inevitably leads to short-term thinking – and before you know it, you've taken your eye off the business ball. Suddenly your thoughts are filled with big houses, fast cars, and life spent on a beach sipping a Piña Colada, rather than how you are going to grow your business.

Added to that is the dilemma of when to sell out: do you take money on the table now or hold on until you have a bigger, better, more profitable business and will make more money on the deal? Suddenly your board are so busy creating spreadsheets working out the value of their share options under this scenario or that scenario, that they forget all about key projects or targets or actually getting anything done. Greed sets in.

When you decide to start actually exploring one of the juicy offers, you will find before long that you are spending more time in meetings with advisors, lawyers and accountants to negotiate, discuss and fine-tune the deal, than you are spending on methods to actually progress your company's turnover or profitability. Fees suddenly start to mount, everyone is focused on microwaving short-term profitability (at the expense of long-term growth), and rumours abound amongst the staff that the company is about to be sold or merged or taken over, all of which can have an incredibly destabilising effect.

At Red Letter Days we received more than a dozen offers over the years from companies who wanted to acquire us in some way. The first was in the mid 1990s and (strangely) came from Green Flag, who were sitting on a heap of money they didn't know what to do with and put forward £1million. It was our first offer, and it just seemed a bit too early to be cashing in – the business was just taking off and actually we were having so much fun running it that we really didn't want to sell out.

Then in the late 1990s Nicola Foulston arrived on our doorstep; her Brands Hatch Leisure Group had been floated and she was under pressure from the City to 'do deals'. The carrot dangled there was £1million each for my and my first husband (who was then CEO), plus an earn-out clause, which at the time seemed quite tempting. But all was left dead in the water when Nicola told us a condition of the deal would be that said husband would not be required post deal – something his ego could not take, unfortunately, and so negotiations quickly collapsed, much to Nicola's annoyance.

Then several approaches came in quick succession, but nothing to really excite us until 2002, when a leisure company called Holidaybreak came knocking at the door. 'Experiences' were the big growth sector in the tourism market; our new CEO had come from the travel sector and they were keen to get in on the action. We were the perfect fit for their business portfolio, and I had a real sense that this was a deal which would actually complete.

I had just stepped back from the business into a non-exec chairman role; I'd been running the business for well over a decade and if I am honest looking back, I really didn't enjoy Red Letter Days any more. It was getting too big, too problematic and too stressful. There were daily hassles to contend with: from big customers, the staff, projects, even just trying to get simple things done. Problems which, when we were a young business, we would have decided on in the morning and implemented by the afternoon, now required a project manager, a Project Initiation Document and a three-month implementation process.

We'd just had one of our most successful years in 2001, when we'd delivered *c.* £1million profit from £10million turnover – which meant the company was probably worth around £10million at that time – and I could easily have imagined being quite happy with my £5million share of that figure. It was enough capital for the other business ideas which I started to dream of pursuing. Focus began to be lost.

So we started the disposal process using our new auditors. They persuaded us that we would be able to negotiate a much, much bigger deal if we went into a full marketing process rather than just focusing on the deal on the table. They wanted to get several parties interested and start a bidding war.

Sensible advice, but it came from a partner who was charging £600 per hour (yes, you've read that correctly!) and who, at that price, must have needed a few extra clients in his portfolio.

We decided to go for it, and teams of expensive accountants began working on our internal due diligence, so that we could prepare the Tender for Sale documentation to put out to the market. The directors (all of whom had big share-option packages) started getting excited; their attention went completely off the job at hand and that Christmas (2002) we failed to meet our new, aggressive sales targets by more than 50%.

Actually, in real terms, it was a really good Christmas, but sadly not nearly enough to support the hugely increased operating costs of the bigger, more ambitious business which had been built in by our new CEO.

Worse was to come: our auditors had discovered serious accounting problems during their review which needed to be resolved, and essentially the Holidaybreak deal (plus the chance of generating any more like it) was left dead in the water. Plus we were left with an accountancy bill of more than £250,000.

To add insult to injury, the auditors started advising the CEO (who had presided over this sorry disaster) that now would be a good time to mount a management buyout against me – his £600-per-hour fees paid for by, yes you've guessed it, yours truly. Utterly outrageous and totally unprofessional.

Exit CEO and exit FD, re-enter Rachel – by this point seven months pregnant – to try to salvage something of the sorry mess.

One of my fellow Dragons, Doug Richard, also fell foul of the perils of a flawed exit strategy, following his rise to success in California. Doug started out in business with his brother in 1986 in the computer hardware sector. He openly admits that at that time neither of them really had a clue what they were doing, nor any great business acumen; they simply saw that computers were the 'next big thing'. They desperately needed to make some money and saw selling hardware as an easy way to cash in on a growing market.

Despite having no real business infrastructure or supply chain, nor indeed any administrative support at all, they rather audaciously pitched for a hardware supply contract which they miraculously managed to partially win – and hey presto, ITAL Computers was up and running.

Seeing that the supply of software held more promise than trading hardware, five years later they sold that first business and, using the capital, set up a second company, Visual Software. Again, riding on the crest of the technology wave, pretty soon this business started to attract attention from the big players, who by this point were buying up boutique IT companies as if there were no tomorrow.

One of those suitors was Micrografx, a huge public company, whose CEO persuaded Doug to do a paper-for-paper deal in 1996 on the promise of big returns under the umbrella of his healthy and profitable business.

Frequently, CEOs in desperate situations will do any deal they can to shore up their own businesses. When you're being courted by what seems like a successful big, publicly floated company, it's easy to omit doing your own reverse due diligence – and miss the fact that there may already be trouble brewing at your new parent-to-be.

Just 85 days after the deal had gone through, the share price of Micrografx plummeted by 99%.

Doug later said of his nightmare: 'I really wish I had taken cash for that company. That was a huge mistake to make. I was back to broke, but I had a lot of shares. I could have papered all the walls in my house with them – and with hindsight, perhaps I should have!'

Fuming with rage, refusing to be beaten, and knowing that the CEO who had been so persuasive was now in an extremely precarious position, Doug corralled the other shareholders and launched a hostile attack on the board, resulting in his own appointment as CEO.

'I then took great pleasure in sacking every last one of the bastards who misled me.'

He then focused on turning round the company's fortunes and eventually sold the company at the height of the dot com boom to Corel in 2001.

It took five years, plus huge amounts of hard work, grit and determination, for Doug to recover his 'lost' fortune. All of which might have been avoided had he refused the paper deal and taken cash instead.

Knowing everything I know now, here's what I would advise you to do if you want to sell your business:

- There are a few exceptions to this rule, but generally speaking your business is most likely to be bought if it is growing and profitable. So, whatever happens and right up to the point of doing the deal, growth and profitability should be your first focus.
- If you are contemplating selling your business, make sure that every aspect of it is rock solid, including its systems, strategy, IP, contracts, accounting policy and people. No area will be overlooked in the due diligence process, and if you aren't proved squeaky clean you can be sure it will be used against you.
- Avoid any form of buyout clause. They are easily manipulated by your new parent company and could even act as a disincentive for your new parent to give you the support you thought you were doing the deal for in the first place.
- Yes, the best time to sell a business is at the height of its value – but how do you know when that time has come? A better yardstick is to sell your business the moment you have lost your passion for it. Selling out will give you the freedom plus the capital you need to do your next business venture
- Get the best advice money can buy, including advisors to help you negotiate the deal. You'll maximise the price that way, and sometimes creating distance from the negotiating table can be a powerful thing.

- Don't be too eager or show too much enthusiasm. In the same way that a man will come on to a woman much harder if she holds back a little in the dating process, sometimes 'going quiet on a deal' for a few days or even weeks can make the other party even more hungry to complete. Sometimes there is nothing more effective than 'radio silence'.

- The more options you have (including the option *not* to sell), the more powerful your hand.

- Try not to value your business based on what you think it is worth. Value it on what it could be worth to the acquiring party – frequently this is a much larger sum than the one in your own mind. Don't sell yourself short.

- Remember, the deal is not done until the ink is on the paper. Until that moment, you cannot assume anything, whatever positive noises are being made or whatever assurances you may be given. To protect yourself in case the deal does go through, do not take your eye off the business ball, and always keep at least three options open.

- In paper-for-paper deals you will always be at the mercy of forces you cannot control, and your lock-in period will often prevent you from disposing of the shares for two years. Therefore always take cash, no matter how tempting the share-for-share option might seem.

6

WHEN PROBLEMS GET PERSONAL

One of the great things about being commissioned to write a book is that it gives you the perfect excuse to actually meet some of your all-time heroes. And so interviewing Jeffrey Archer was more of a personal indulgence for me than a logical inclusion for a book on entrepreneurship. Wealth creator? Most certainly yes. Entrepreneur? Most probably no.

However, Jeffrey Archer was the strongest and earliest influence on my own entrepreneurial journey. I remember playing truant from school, aged 14, and sitting at home watching him being interviewed on a daytime chat show, stating most emphatically, 'You will never make money working for anyone else'. Of course, at the age of 14 I didn't have a clue what I wanted to do with my life – I only knew what I didn't want to do, and that was go to school. But the memory of that interview always stuck with me, especially through my early jobs in accountancy, stuck in airless offices, ploughing through mountains of filing, earning less per year than I now do for making a 30-minute speech.

Of course, Jeffrey Archer's life has been a roller coaster since that TV interview back in 1976. He is, after all, a supreme risk taker, like the rest of the entrepreneurs in this book. But, as I found to my personal cost (in a much smaller way of course), when you are a high-flying, high-profile risk taker there is an absolute army of faceless, jealous people out there, just ready to use whatever tiny pocket of power they may possess to bring you down.

Our interview is scheduled to take place at Jeffrey's penthouse apartment overlooking the Thames. On my arrival, the lift takes me to the top floor and opens directly into the hallway of the apartment, where Jeffrey's butler is waiting.

The room is stunning – white marble and cream sofas, with objets d'art everywhere and a mountain of art books on the coffee table in front of us. Plus of course the incredible views through the double-height floor-to-ceiling windows – to the Houses of Parliament and every London landmark beyond to one side, and Chelsea Embankment to the other.

Those first five seconds of any meeting always energetically set the tone for what is to follow, but any nerves I may have had evaporate in the warmth of the sheer charisma and positive energy that surrounds the man.

Jeffrey opens by asking how I found working with Duncan Bannatyne – my co-star on the first two series of *Dragons' Den* and his on ITV's *Fortune: Million Pound Giveaway*. My simple laugh is the green light for Jeffrey to express his forthright views on Duncan (the ultimate clash of alpha-male egos, by the sound of it), which proves to be the ice-breaker to a fascinating hour-long interview.

Jeffrey tells me about his earliest enterprise – going down to his local train station in the West Country with a pram and taking people's luggage to their guest house for sixpence.

'I was taking back to my school 30 shillings – that's £1.50 – which was a vast amount of money in a schoolboy's pocket. My mother never knew anything about this but I was arriving in school as the rich boy; it never crossed my mind then that I was an entrepreneur.'

But every account of Jeffrey's early life highlights his self-belief, determination and drive – the three prerequisite qualities of the successful entrepreneur. In response to being teased at school about his physique, he embarked on rigorous weight training and gymnastics. He went on to become games master at Dover College, which backed him to become a mature student at Oxford University, where he gained an athletics Blue, and the friends who would go on to become MPs, City financiers and newspaper editors.

After a spell at the Greater London Council, Jeffrey fulfilled his political ambitions by being elected as Tory MP for the safe seat of Louth in Lincolnshire, at his third attempt.

By his early thirties, Jeffrey was riding high, a successful MP with a home in Kensington and all the trappings of wealth.

They say that you are at your most vulnerable in business when everything is going well – you start to think you have the Midas touch and become over confident. So disaster struck for Jeffrey when he invested in a Canadian company, Aquablast, believing that the company held intellectual property rights which would make it (and him) a fortune. But it was a scam which led to a high-profile legal case in Canada, and Jeffrey lost his entire £350,000 investment. The problem was, the original money to invest in the business came from money Jeffrey had borrowed and now had no means of repaying.

'I have never met a multi-millionaire in my life who hasn't lost everything before. Never. The secret is to never mention it. Jimmy Goldsmith was a good friend of mine – he lost millions and millions; but he made it back in other ways. He put large sums into ventures he thought couldn't fail but they did. We've all done it.' (See Chapter 17)

'I faced bankruptcy but was never actually declared bankrupt. I was insolvent to the tune of £430,000 – a lot of money in 1974. But my debts were owed to the tax man and to one person, who were both willing to wait. Most people go under if they have 100 bills they can't pay; I had two big ones and I went to them and negotiated and they agreed, and it took me seven years to pay them back.'

Realising the scandal of his over-stretched position, Jeffrey resigned as an MP and was effectively unemployed, with no clear route by which he could work his way out of the financial meltdown. 'It was my books that paid the creditors back, but quite unintentionally. I started writing, not intending to make any money at all but just to make sure my son could see that I was busy at least working on something while I was unemployed.

'I presented my first book, *Not a Penny More, Not a Penny Less*, to publishing houses without having a deal beforehand. The first 17 turned it down; the 18th gave me £3,000 – which didn't make a very big dent in £400,000. And when it launched it only sold 3,000 copies on its first year.

'It was my third book, *Kane and Abel*, which made me the money. The story had been made into a mini series for TV, and so when the book was released it sold a million copies in its first week. I was literally overdrawn on the Monday and a millionaire on the Tuesday. I'm the most nouveau riche person you've ever met – you don't get rich faster than that!'

After *Kane and Abel* Jeffrey's world changed overnight. He and his wife Mary moved out of their rented flat in Cambridge and bought The Old Vicarage the next week, where they have lived ever since.

'I didn't ever think that I could write a fourth book, or a fifth book, but I just kept getting ideas for more stories. I write because I love it; I don't have to work any more – I write because I want to write.'

It's at this point that Jeffrey questions me on how I intend to write THIS book, upon which I have to admit that it isn't a matter to which I've actually given much thought. But perhaps I should have done – because I can tell you now (while sitting here under pressure of my third extended publisher's deadline) that it is far more difficult than it looks. Especially with five children (including a new-born baby) to contend with, and a business to run. So Jeffrey shares with me the secret of his book-writing regime.

'I have a ruthless discipline. I spend a year thinking

about my next book, planning it in my head. Then I fly out on 28 December each year to my villa in Majorca to write it. On 1 March I fly home with the completed manuscript. The story is complete but I then work on tightening the copy, making every page one you want to turn, going through everything at least 10 times to get to the final version I'm happy with.'

His results are impressive: 14 novels, three plays, five sets of short stories and three prison diaries, written in a career spanning over 30 years, published in 63 countries and in more than 32 languages, with international sales of over 130 million copies. All of which has gone towards making Jeffrey Archer rich beyond his wildest dreams.

Yes, there have been trials (quite literally) and tribulations along the way, but having met the man, I couldn't envisage his life being anything other than a roller-coaster ride of the most amazing experiences – some good, some bad.

So I have revisited my judgement. Entrepreneur? No. Ultrapreneur? Most definitely yes (see page 206 for more on Ultrapreneurs).

I came away from my meeting with Jeffrey totally recharged and enthused by his infectious energy and inspiration. He showed me that even in your darkest hour of despair, wonderful new paths and opportunities can emerge which will take you in a totally new and much more fulfilling direction. I know from my own experience of living through the nightmare meltdown of Red Letter Days, as a result of which I lost 16 years of my life which I had invested to build the company up, that the moment I let go, all sorts of wonderful new opportunities started to emerge for me – including being offered the deal to write this book.

So, if you experience yourself going through a crisis, whether in business or in life, have faith that something very amazing will ultimately come out of it – even if it's difficult to see it at the time.

My personal insights if you are facing a business or financial meltdown:

- Stop fighting the adversity and go with the flow – one chapter in life has to end before another can begin. Learn to let go.
- Say 'yes' to new opportunities and offers, even if you can't immediately see how they might be of help. The magic can't happen unless you open the door when someone starts knocking.
- Seek fresh inspiration through books, films and new experiences – the future is a blank canvas that you can paint it any way you want.
- Cut loose from any negative influences from your past that are bringing you down and seek the company of new, positive people. Your crisis will show you who your real friends are.
- No matter how black the current outlook is, hold on to your dream of how you would like life to be when you come out of the tunnel. Stay positive and you will attract exactly the people and opportunities you need to get you out of your current situation.

7

THE DANGER OF GOING INTERNATIONAL

Call me a xenophobe, but I have always had a great fear of going international in business. The option was always there with Red Letter Days; actually, it really was the logical thing to do – one, because the range of experiences available within the UK is so limited and two, because the weather here is so dire. I figured that if we could offer a white-water rafting voucher which you could use at venues in England, Wales and Scotland, then how difficult would it be to add the Colorado River, the Alps and Australia into the choices? OK, there may not have been many redemptions, but it sure would have made our product range much sexier and would also have increased our ability to sell into the corporate market. Plus we could then add on all sorts of things like international travel and accommodation, and before you knew it we would be the world's number one experiences company.

But fear of the unknown (not to mention the fact that we had major problems just trying to cope with the growth of our UK operation) kept me stuck to UK experiences – and to what I knew best.

Immediately after the crash of Red Letter Days I knew that working in the UK experiences sector was simply not an option for me. But I was approached by several overseas experiences companies who wanted me to help them develop their businesses. I had no real desire to get involved in the experiences sector again, but frankly, I needed the consultancy income. So, over time, I built up a portfolio of experiences company contacts in the USA, South America, Australia, Europe and the Middle East – and eventually it dawned on me that maybe creating an international experiences network might not be so difficult after all.

For a while I had been in contact with a guy called Antonio Quina, who had always been a fan of what I had done in the UK and had created his Portuguese experiences company, Avida e Bela (Life is Beautiful), almost entirely based on the Red Letter Days model. With Antonio's help I set up an 'international summit' of experiences companies in Lisbon, in an attempt to kick off an international network. Antonio managed to persuade a 5-star luxury golf resort and spa to provide us with free accommodation, and so all our international partners had to do was get themselves to Lisbon and listen to what we had to say.

As the weekend rolled on it quickly became apparent that trying to get everyone to work together was going to be very difficult. For a start, there were fundamental differences in the way we all thought the international network should be structured. I believed we should create an international group using share-for-share deals which we would quickly be able to float, giving all parties a properly funded umbrella under which they could each develop their businesses. Each company could then share the same resources, including a global experiences booking network via the web which would allow users to browse and book experiences anywhere in the world. But Antonio and his team preferred a joint-venture model where essentially they would license their marketing collateral and existing systems to each member – really just a way of generating additional revenue streams for their own already established business.

When it became obvious that there was no meeting of minds, much to everyone's shock, one of Antonio's partners privately set about poaching each and every company I had brought to our little 'summit'. I actually found this quite amusing, as I had already made it a condition of each consultancy contract that I would have first option to work with the company in an international venture, and could therefore block them from working with Antonio's team. One thing I learned from that experience is that northern Europeans seem to be a bit more ethical in their approach to business, whereas it would seem that our Latin friends are perhaps not.

As the weekend wore on, tensions mounted. While the south Europeans got more and more angry, the north Europeans got more and more drunk; the Brazilians thought the creative tension was pretty cool (too much Semco influence can be a bad thing), while the preppy boys from Colorado – and their cheer-leader-like wives – looked on in bewilderment. The only people who didn't seem that fazed were the Israelis – but then they were used to working in Tel Aviv.

So that was the end of my small brush with 'going international'; it is extremely difficult to make business work when you are trying to work across different cultures, language barriers and ways of doing business.

And so it was with interest that earlier this year I read an interview in *The Daily Telegraph* about how Brian Souter, who co-founded the incredibly successful Stagecoach Group, which is now one of Britain's biggest transport companies, almost lost it all by expanding into the USA.

Stagecoach was one of the huge success stories of the 1980s.

Scottishborn Brian had been born on a Perth council estate and his father was a bus driver. When he was at university, Brian took a job as a bus conductor to make ends meet.

In the interview Brian said: 'I always tried to work out the economics of the buses. One Monday morning I worked out I had collected £240 (at 1977 prices), and my wages were £29 a week. What happened to the rest? I figured there must be some margin in buses.'

Souter seized the opportunity to create his own bus company in 1980, when Margaret Thatcher deregulated long-distance bus routes. He teamed up with his sister, Ann Gloag, and using his father's redundancy cheque of £25,000 they bought two buses. 'It was horribly hard work and very scary. We were over-trading, under-capitalised and completely exhausted. We answered phones through the night alternately between us for six years.' They were selling a Glasgow-to-London fare at £7, and needed every penny they could get.

From that small start the business grew, with Stagecoach acquiring more and more buses and routes, and then later acquiring various train franchises.

By 2000 profits stood at over £200million and the business was doing very nicely indeed. But the company had just acquired an overseas subsidiary in a deal worth £1.2billion – a company called Coach USA – which proved to be the acquisition that would risk the entire business.

Brian later admitted that he should have done more due diligence when acquiring the company – its auditors were from the same firm that went on to infamy as Enron's auditors. 'Coach USA was different from what we had done in the past in that it had a lot more leisure businesses in it. That was the weakness. The first year's trading was significantly below forecast. Then our luck ran out.

'Sure, there were valuation, trading and management issues, but nothing we couldn't have worked our way out of if it hadn't been for 9/11. The US leisure business evaporated overnight. My intuition after we had bought it was that we had made a mistake. It was in too many different geographies and areas. We should have gone for a structural solution much sooner.'

Stagecoach's profits crashed to a £500million loss in 2002 and its share price collapsed to just over 10 pence.

By this point Brian had stepped back into a chairman's role and Keith Cochrane, the chief executive, departed over the debacle, leaving Souter to take over the CEO reins. He swiftly disposed of the majority of Coach USA and took a £940million write-off, which restored the City's faith in the company.

Souter then refocused on the company's UK activities, acquiring the East Midlands rail franchise and bringing the company back into profitability.

Profitability has since been restored and last year the company delivered £180million profit from a turnover of £1.5billion. The share price is now a healthy £2.91 and the company has a market capitalisation of over £2billion. Plenty of growth to go for in the UK then, without ever having to look towards the international market.

There are numerous examples of companies who have been burned by developing their business overseas – Marks & Spencer and Pret A Manger to name just two. Others have pulled it off, but in my opinion, international expansion has to be one area that could easily turn into your biggest business nightmare.

Here are my observations on successfully taking your business international, based on my own limited experience, plus everything I've ever heard or read on the subject:

- Make sure you have your home market absolutely sewn up first.
- Find a top-class local management team which understands the culture of your target country and how business is done there. Trust them to run the business the way they believe it should be done, and put in place bulletproof management reporting, to enable you to monitor things from a distance.
- Be very careful to control the cash (as per Michelle Mone's experience in Chapter 4).
- Get some top-quality advisers on board; people who know every pitfall of what you are planning – this is one area where you do not want to be learning by experience.
- Consider franchising as a low-risk option.

8

DON'T LOSE CONTROL OF YOUR BABY

One of the people I most wanted to interview for this book was the late, great Dame Anita Roddick. She was one of my greatest entrepreneurial influences as a young career girl working in the City in the 1980s, when power women like Anita, Debbie Moore (Pineapple) and Sophie Mirman (Sock Shop) exploded onto the business scene.

I remember driving home from a business meeting late one Monday night, when the shocking news came over the radio that Anita had died of a brain haemorrhage. This news was followed closely by a call from the BBC asking if I would go on breakfast TV to talk about Anita's influence as the highest-profile female entrepreneur Britain has ever seen. I could not do the TV show, but the next day I did participate in an interview for City A.M.'s daily webcast, which I barely managed to finish because I was so choked with tears.

Roll back the clock to a 'women in business' event four years earlier at Mosimann's private dining rooms in London, where I had accepted an invitation to hear Anita speak. She was a great draw, the room was packed and the glitterati of female entrepreneurship were there, including Michelle Mone (Ultimo), Linda Bennett (LK Bennett), Julie Meyer (First Tuesday), Sahar Hashemi (Coffee Republic) as well as up-and-coming stars like Sally Preston (Babylicious).

My overriding memory of the event was the sheer power of the way her words were delivered. Afterwards, during questions (by which time the room was virtually vibrating with the amount of energy generated – an energy I have only ever experienced at female-only events), I asked Anita the question which held a burning fascination for me as an observer of her business empire, at the time I was busy building my own: 'At what point did you lose control of your business?'

A strange question, but she knew exactly what I meant and immediately said it was in 1992 – a year which must have been burned on her mind. By that point her company, The Body Shop, which she had created at her kitchen table in 1976, had been floated on the London Stock Exchange, was riding high internationally, and was a multi-million-pound money-making machine. Anita had wanted to use The Body Shop's power to launch yet another international political campaign. But the board had voted against her.

Anita went on to pioneer the campaign in her own name, but it was clear from the surrounding media coverage that instead of being viewed as an asset to The Body Shop, Anita was starting to be seen as something of an embarrassment, whose influence needed to be controlled and curtailed rather than nurtured and encouraged. Thus the slow death of the brand began.

I have always maintained that women approach business very differently to men. Whereas men's primary motivation for being in business is to make money, women tend to make a business out of something they have a great passion for. In Anita's case it was cosmetics made from natural ingredients which were not tested on animals and which were sourced ethically from the Third World. She was way ahead of her time in every respect, in an era when the trend in business was going in totally the opposite direction – maximisation of profit and manufacturing efficiency, whatever the human or environmental cost.

Men tend to be 'serial entrepreneurs', looking at which sectors hold the most profit potential, extracting as much value as possible, as quickly as possible, and then moving on to the next money-making mine. But for Anita and many other women like her, her business was her passion, the 'magnum opus' of her life, the thing that she poured every last part of herself into. Women do not create companies, they give birth to them.

So, when you lose control of your baby (no matter how much money you make in the process), it is excruciatingly painful.

The problem with any form of outside intervention or ownership in business – and in particular anything involving corporate financiers or the City – is that immediately on signing you find yourself in the hands of the 'alpha males'. The alpha males only care about your passion so long as it adds to their bottom line, for profit is all they are interested in – and profit in the form of interim and final results at that. A six-month horizon, for a business which has the potential to thrive for a lifetime. As I have mentioned before, what is so damaging about having such a short-term results horizon is that the temptation to microwave profits is huge – sacrificing long-term value for short-term gain.

The problem with the alpha-male approach is that it is so obsessed with COST that it loses sight of VALUE – and that is when the rot sets in. It is in this way that the magic of so many great entrepreneurial brands has been eroded and ultimately destroyed over time.

But the great dilemma in trying to expand a business to the point where it can have a worldwide influence is that ultimately you do need to seek external finance and funding, even though you may end up selling your soul to the devil in the process.

I never did manage to ask Anita, but I suspect that she was deeply against selling her baby to L'Oréal – even though it netted her £130million. For L'Oréal is a company which represents almost everything The Body Shop was against, and is also part-owned by Nestlé – one of the most boycotted companies in the world.

Inevitably, customers are sceptical and within days of the deal, The Body Shop's rating on the YouGov BrandIndex was in freefall, with consumers not convinced by announcements that L'Oréal intended to retain all of its new subsidiary's ethical policies. The buyout turned out to be a brand disaster.

There was nothing Anita could have done to block the L'Oréal deal, even if she had wanted to, because once you lose control of your business you never get it back again. The alpha males had smelled money, and it seemed to them that success could only be measured in fiscal terms.

The parallel to my own business experience is obvious, although the circumstances were dramatically different (and I didn't receive £130million to cushion the blow!). But exactly like Anita, I lost control of my business after investing 16 years of my life in it.

For one thing, seeing the brand you have created and nurtured for so many years being run by people with a pure profit motive and who do not understand the brand's DNA is actually quite heartbreaking. It's also saddening because, under its new ownership, even though new life may have temporarily been breathed in, you know that your creation will ultimately wither and die.

A businesswoman must let go, because often her business is the platform which allows her to pursue much higher and worthier ambitions. In Anita's case, these were the human rights initiatives which she devoted her last years to. By the time that she died, Anita was no longer a businesswoman: she was a Warrior Queen.

If you want to make sure you keep control of your business then I suggest you:

- Hang on to your equity at all costs. Once you sell shares it is very difficult to get them back again.
- Grow organically – even if it takes longer. This also makes for a much more stable, robust business.
- Remember profit is the best form of cash injection. Everything you do in business should be in a constant effort to improve the bottom line, but never at the expense of your brand.
- Don't issue share options to your staff. They're a one-way street which, in truth, the vast majority of people don't actually value nearly as much as cash in hand – and the reality is that very few people within your business, acting alone, can materially affect the bottom line. If you feel you must share the success with staff, use individually performance-linked profit-sharing schemes instead.
- Avoid all forms of corporate finance – whether through banks, venture capitalists or stock market listings – or you could find yourself dancing to the devil's tune.

9

BEWARE THE ENEMIES WITHIN

One of the great things about being a 'celebrity entrepreneur' is that you get invited to lots of business events and are normally seated at the top table – rubbing shoulders with Captains of Industry, other high-profile entrepreneurs and various other Very Important People.

It was at such an event in Edinburgh that I met the MP for Central Ayrshire, the charming Brian Donohoe – a devoted Brownite, who (despite my publicly declared allegiance to David Cameron) invited me to lunch at the House of Commons as his guest, after which he gave me a 'behind the scenes' tour of the Houses of Parliament.

As we were making our way down one of the corridors of MPs' offices, Brian said a friendly 'hello' to a passing Tory MP, upon which I expressed shock that he was being friendly with 'the enemy'. 'No Rachel,' Brian pointed out. 'Your enemies in politics are not on the other side of the House – they're within your own party.'

Proving his words, there followed in quick succession no fewer than three political oustings: Charles Kennedy betrayed by certain Liberal Democrat MPs because of his problems with alcohol, Blair booted out in favour of Brown, and then Sir Menzies Campbell effectively forced to resign, only months after being appointed as Liberal Democrat leader, due to his unpopularity in the polls.

As it is in politics, so it is in business.

Most entrepreneurs I know are highly trusting, eternal optimists, and so it is incredibly easy to naively believe that you are building a strong and loyal board of directors – only to have them turn on you the moment they sniff money and the greed sets in. This is exactly what happened to my friend Al Gosling, founder of the Extreme TV Sports Channel, which now broadcasts in 60 countries worldwide.

Al is a real people person, one of those rare businessmen driven primarily by his passion for his business and not the desire for material wealth. A 'Passionpreneur' (see page 206 for more on this), he still doesn't own a house, his only car is in Switzerland and he travels in the UK by bike. Above all, Al is highly trusting of his team.

Here's how that trust was repaid.

'I was 24 and really wanted to do something for myself; at the beginning the vision was a mix of sport and business because I love those two things. I wanted to build a great company, with a bunch of good people. I wanted to build something reasonably big.

'I started out in business in 1995. We built a TV distribution business, an agent for sports programmes.

So if you were a TV producer in Canada or Spain or wherever, you'd make a series about snowboarding or surfing or multi-sport. You might sell it in your territory and then you would give us the international rights and we would sell it globally for you. At the same time as we continued to trade, we built up a huge library of footage. We didn't own it all but we had control of it.

'By 1998 we had built up thousands and thousands of hours of programmes, and it was at that point that I had the idea to combine it all into a TV channel. So I bought the web domain 'extreme.com' for $32,000 from a guy at Microsoft (who was using it for pictures of his cat and Ferrari), we created the Extreme logo, and on 1 May 1999, we launched the Extreme TV Sports Channel in Holland.'

Al then stopped running the TV distribution business and started running the TV channel business for the next two and a half years. He took it from one country to 39 countries, a gruelling task, which involved a lot of European travel.

Then, in a classic example of a boardroom coup against the entrepreneurial founder of the business, Al found himself faced by his finance director (who had been put in by earlier investors in the business), who alleged that the business was about to suffer a major cash flow crisis.

The FD and several other members of his board urged that the business needed a further equity injection of £500,000. Six weeks before they thought the company needed this money, they offered to invest, in a deal where Al's 68% controlling stake would be reduced to 30%, giving the investors the majority stake in the business.

Another condition of the deal was that Al had to step down as CEO.

'They probably didn't think they needed me. I had been abroad so much that I had taken my finger off the pulse of the business. I was quite wet behind the ears, I had built the business up and then it seemed like these guys were trying to sideswipe me. I can only think that greed blinded them; they could see that the business was beginning to take off and they wanted the lion's share of it. I lost my business innocence in an instant.

'Just six weeks prior I had actually been one of 40 guests at the private wedding in the south of France of one of those involved. One of the directors on the board was a ruthless corporate investor but the rest were really, really close friends. I felt completely betrayed. That was the absolute low point in business for me.'

In situations like this it is wise to receive counsel from people outside the company who are completely independent and who have nothing to gain, and so Al sought the advice of an experienced businessman who had himself been stitched up many times.

'I had sleepless nights, and endured four months of the hardest work I have ever done. But I managed to hang on and managed to get myself out of the situation. It was my Shareholders' Agreement that saved me – plus my gritty and very hard determination not to be beaten.'

The board members threatened that if Al did not agree to the deal, they were going to release a press statement the following Monday stating they were all resigning because of a disagreement amongst the board. But Al would not be frightened into submission. He called on some friends at Brunswick (the corporate PR company) and asked for their help. He had no cash to pay them (because he thought the company was broke) but they still agreed to intervene.

'They said: "That's cool, give us half a day to construct the most hardcore press statement imaginable in response to theirs which, if published, will be the first thing that comes up every time any one of these guys gets Googled." They told me: "You're at war, and in war it's who has got the balls to be one step ahead that wins."'

The company's corporate lawyer stepped in to support Al and insisted he too did not want any form of payment. He ended up working constantly for four months alongside Al to fight the board.

'With these allies on my side, I then pushed the finance director straight out of the main business into one of our retail subsidiaries and personally took control of the company cheque book. In an attempt to control cash flow, no payment went out of that company without my authority for four months. It caused absolute chaos. What was amazing was that for eight or nine years we had been paying suppliers across our entire business on the nail, so the amount of goodwill we had built up allowed us to stretch supplier payments. Meanwhile I worked to raise the money I believed the business needed.'

Al managed to raise £300,000 within four weeks, which was put into their lawyer's client account to use as leverage against the rest of the board. But in the end, this money was never used. It transpired that the business did not actually need any extra financing and Al feels that the cash flow crisis had been exaggerated as a scare tactic to try to force the deal through.

'Once the situation was averted I thought: How badly do I nail these guys to the wall? Board meetings from then on were pretty frosty and one by one I removed every last one of those guys from the board. I then sold the TV channel side of the business and used the money to buy out those of the traitors who were also shareholders and to regain 100% ownership of the company. But I actually did a very reasonable deal with them, I didn't nail them completely, I really didn't, I was actually quite soft.

'It's just very sad when people whom you trust start smelling the money and turn on you.'

But every cloud has a silver lining, and Al has since gone on to extend the Extreme brand into drinks, retail, clothing, events, mobile, pre-pay cards, travel, electronics, hotels and theme parks. Currently, the Extreme Group employs more than 250 people and is represented in 70 countries around the world.

And, to his credit, Al still has incredible trust in his new team, ensuring that everyone has share options in the business plus a slice of the profits each year.

Al's is a sad but sobering business nightmare that every entrepreneur should take heed of. It is true that as you grow you do need to build a great, talented team around you, but at the same time you need to be very, very careful whom you allow on to your board, lest they use their power against you.

The most important of these is your finance director, who has the most power of all – especially if you are not particularly numbers savvy. In fact, based on some of the conversations I have had with other entrepreneurs, I could probably write an entire book of business nightmares based purely on finance directors.

My own experience of abuse of board power also involved my FD and my chairman trying to push through a refinancing deal, under which they each stood to take 5% of the company for no investment, once again on the basis of ultra conservative cash flows. On that occasion, on the advice of a friend who was a corporate financier, I succeeded in persuading the majority of the board to remove the chairman, as a result of which the FD immediately walked out.

His replacement proceeded to unlock £3million of cash back into the business within six weeks – simple things like collecting on trade debtors (we were owed over £1million – much of which was over 60 days old) and renegotiating settlement terms (we were paying suppliers within 14 days of invoice).

Fear is a great motivator – and if people are forcing you to make decisions based on fear it's usually a sign that you are being tricked. So choose an FD not just on the technical ability demonstrated by his CV: choose someone whom you can trust with your life.

Many entrepreneurs find it difficult to make the transition from being the sole director of their company to creating a proper board (bear in mind you really only need to do this if you are trying to bring in external finance). Here are my tips for creating a board which adds value, yet is still manageable and controllable:

- Limit the number of executive directors to the absolute minimum needed to be effective. Even some of the largest companies often only have a managing director, a finance director and a sales/marketing or operations director, supplemented by two or three non-execs. Remember, a board is there to set the strategy of the business, not to be the operational team.
- Appoint any non-execs yourself – choosing people both whose opinions you value and who are likely to support you if it comes to the crunch.
- Don't allow any director to persuade you to recruit their friends or ex-colleagues on to the board; you could be building a power base against you.
- Make it a condition of the Shareholders' Agreement that you cannot be removed as an executive director of the company while you hold any more than 10% of the shares in the business.
- If any director starts acting against your interests as a majority shareholder (unless required to do so by their duties under the Companies Act, which is generally if

the company is insolvent and must switch to making decisions in the interests of the creditors), remove them while you still have the power to do so.

- If fear of insolvency is being used to lever you out, make sure you obtain expert independent external advice: get a second opinion.
- Make sure that your FD is not only technically brilliant, but also someone you can really trust.

10

FOCUS ON YOUR CUSTOMERS NOT YOUR COMPETITORS

After what can seem like an eternity of struggle in the darkness, as you will see James Dyson found in Chapter 13, eventually there comes the wonderful day when your business finally starts to take off. You're now attracting customers like bees to the proverbial honey, money is flowing and suddenly the press is starting to pay you attention.

No matter what sector you're in, sooner or later you are bound to be eyed jealously. This may come from lazy opportunists who decide to take the easy route and try to rip off your business idea, or from existing players in your sector who, driven by their own fear and insecurity of losing market share, start to divert their energy from running their own business to trying to undermine yours.

Fear of competitors is a curiously male phenomenon. Where women tend to welcome newcomers into their industry, men tend to despise them. That's because most women are Passionpreneurs who actually embrace collaboration – an approach based on positivity, not fear, and which ultimately leads to much stronger businesses in the long run (see page 206 for more on Passionpreneurs).

In fact, I would go so far as to say that if we want to find a solution to the world's problems, it has to be through more feminine ways of working – like collaboration, helping others and trading ethically – rather than the traditional male business instinct to make money by winning at any cost.

The truth is that no one company can ever 'own' an entire sector and if you are smart you actually shouldn't even attempt to try. It is far better to focus on that distinct part of the market where you can really shine, rather than dumbing everything down by trying to be all things to all people. McDonald's always used to have a great saying: 'We focus on our customers, not our competitors' (although even they lost the mantra by becoming too complacent with their menu in the late 1990s). It amazes me how many companies spend their time, energy and focus obsessed with other players in their sector rather than customer-orientated product or service innovation.

Nothing brought this home to me more than my experience creating Red Letter Days. I thought I was simply building a company but in reality I was sparking an entire business sector, which by the end of the 1990s had spawned a whole rash of copycat companies.

At the time I do remember feeling that terrible fear when the really big players started to enter our market – notably WH Smith, who created their Amazing Adventures range and Virgin, who licensed their brand to one of our smaller competitors to create Virgin Experiences. But I shouldn't have worried, because every time a big new player arrived on the scene it simply grew the sector even more – and, as market leader, our own business mushroomed.

The fact was, Red Letter Days was not actually operating in the experiences sector at all (estimated at the time to be worth just £200million – of which we attracted nearly 10%), but in the far larger gifts market, then worth £34billion. So a much better strategy for us was to work out how we could hold our own alongside other premium gift brands (like Tiffany, Sony and Gucci), rather than waste our time bothering too much about the other players in the much smaller experiences market.

What a shame our little competitors did not see it that way. One man , who to my mind was a particularly short-sighted businessman called Angus Grahame, saw what we were doing with Red Letter Days and decided to create his own similar version called Activity Superstore. He seemed to focus all his energy on doing us down.

By the early 2000s the Red Letter Days brand was riding high and although Activity Superstore went head-to-head with us over many big retail contracts, they usually ended up winning the ones we didn't want. We never ceased to be amazed how Activity Superstore would seem to do everything it could to better our proposals, even for what seemed to us to be uncommercial, low-margin deals with downmarket brands. Meanwhile, we kept the prime department store accounts – Harrods, Selfridges, House of Fraser and Debenhams.

So when Red Letter Days had its 'annus horribilus' in 2002/3, I'm sure it was to the great delight of Grahame, who arranged for copies of our accounts, when they were filed at Companies House, to be sent to the buyers at all our major retail clients.

This may on the face of it have seemed like a good strategy, but in reality, it was a huge turn-off for the buyers concerned. Most people in business (and certainly those who work in large corporates) are actually pretty decent, regular people, and I received more than one email saying that they would never deal with a company that stooped so low.

The one retailer who did sit up and listen, though, was our biggest – Debenhams – whom, stupidly, we had allowed to become far too big a customer, and whose £6million annual spend with us represented a third of our turnover. Debenhams used their power over us to get out of their contract with us, both withdrawing agreed purchase orders as well as changing the contracted settlement terms. This became a major factor in our eventual decision to put the company into administration.

This occurred even though they were a major stakeholder in the business and even though I struggled into London to meet with their FD to beg him to help us work together to find a solution, just three days before my fourth son was born.

A week later the business was in administration.

So did Grahame benefit from his actions? Short term, I think he probably thought so: the new owners of Red Letter Days withdrew from the retail sector (fundamentally because it was actually unprofitable), leaving it wide open for Activity Superstore to win all those department store accounts.

Longer term, I think the jury is still out. The crash of Red Letter Days was so high profile that it actually served to damage the consumers' appetite for experience-type gifts as a whole – so they all reverted to buying MP3 players or designer merchandise. According to a recent Mintel report the entire sector has stalled and Activity Superstore, once number two in the market is now languishing in fifth or sixth place. Much like the Farepak hamper company crash which shortly followed it, the demise of Red Letter Days as market leader actually decimated the ENTIRE experiences sector.

So trying to bring your competitors down can actually be a high-risk strategy. Not only do you harm your own brand, you can also tarnish the industry as a whole. Trying to create money by destroying others is also a really negative way to spend your energy and brings with it bad karma.

Take Specsavers, for example, and their reaction to the launch of James Murray Wells' company, Glasses Direct. The young entrepreneur created a huge stir in the sleepy old opticians sector when he launched his audacious Glasses Direct business online in 2004, in direct competition to some very established high street players.

Internet businesses often have minimal overheads, and are therefore able to dramatically undercut traditional retailers on price, which was exactly Jamie's strategy: offering glasses at up to 50% off high street prices.

Yet the optical sector is much more than just a 'commodity supplier'. People want great service, they need reassurance and they also want to know that their eyes are in the hands of people they can trust. All of which is difficult to deliver over the internet.

Of course, in any market there will always be people who will shop on price, but there are also a huge number more who want, above all else, fast, prompt and courteous service. In the opticians' business, part of this includes a great choice of frames to try on, and advice on what suits their face shape or colouring.

There are so many Unique Selling Propositions other than price driving the purchasing decision that I really can't see why the established opticians were bothered by the emergence of Glasses Direct at all. In fact, I can't think of a product I'd be LESS likely to buy over the internet, even if I were totally skint, but then I think I am probably not in Jamie's younger, more online-savvy, price-sensitive target market. But Specsavers saw things differently.

Instead of just letting Glasses Direct try and fail, it intervened by complaining to the regulator that its competitor's glasses were unsafe. This undermined Jamie's business – not just in the eyes of the consumer but within the industry itself. This culminated in attempts to stop Jamie's appointment to the Optometrist Council. Then a blatantly ridiculous legal battle ensued, with Specsavers objecting to Glasses Direct's allegations that Specsavers' glasses were more expensive.

Luckily, Jamie had some good PR and marketing people on his team, who decided to react to all this bully-boy posturing not with fear, but with fun. They famously herded a flock of sheep into a Specsavers shop with placards saying, 'Don't get fleeced' and 'Don't let anyone pull wool over your eyes on price' – while the press had a field day.

So in fact the Specsavers onslaught gave Jamie's business a huge amount of valuable free publicity. Not to mention extra impetus, energy and motivation at a time when the business was actually struggling with lots of problems in all areas, problems which might have caused it to wither away and die quietly of natural causes. A far better response from Specsavers would simply have been to completely ignore Glasses Direct, and instead focus all of its energy on emphasising the USPs of its own business – all the things with which Glasses Direct could never compete.

At the time of writing Glasses Direct is still not making profit, but, thanks to the acres of publicity Specsavers helped them generate via the David *v.* Goliath battle, Jamie has successfully managed to build turnover sufficiently so that now venture capitalists are queuing up to provide the capital needed for Glasses Direct to become a REALLY significant threat to Specsavers.

After all, if the market leader is worried about the sector newcomer, surely that means they have huge potential to ultimately steal market share?

I am not advocating total complacency of course – but at the end of the day it is a far better strategy to focus on what customers want. Everyone will probably say they want it cheaper, but the reality is that for most consumers price is so far down the list of criteria that, provided a business is brilliant at all the other aspects, it shouldn't really ever have to worry about cheaper competitors, whatever sector it is in.

A few insights on competitors:

- You will always have competitors: existing companies if you are entering an established sector; new ones once you have found success with an innovative new concept. There are certain laws that may or may not protect you – and it certainly helps to defend your ideas via patents and trademarks. But your best protection in business is always to be considered as 'the best' by your target customer.
- No single business can ever take an entire business sector, so focus on the market segment that you can be brilliant in.
- Don't assume that your competitors are any smarter than you. In fact, newcomers in a sector can have just as much advantage as existing players because they are not bogged down by 'the way things have always been done'.
- Unless you are a massive player with huge economies of scale (like IKEA or Tesco), don't compete purely on price.
- Spend your energy on finding out what customers want and then giving it to them – not obsessing about what competitors are doing.
- Don't be tempted to copy anyone else. Instead, innovate, innovate, innovate – even at the risk of sometimes failing.

11

WHEN YOU THINK BIG, THE PROBLEMS ARE BIGGER

If you are a follower of my Blog, you will know that I am not exactly a fan of the 'alpha male'. However, the one I *will* make an exception for is 'The Donald' himself.

Donald Trump was a bit of a hero for me back in the 1980s and 1990s – years when I was a career girl in the City and later launching my first business Red Letter Days, when I was a scary 'alpha female' myself. (I didn't start out that way, but I quickly found that if I wanted to get anywhere in the business world I would need to harden up, and fast. It wasn't until success had started flowing – which brings its own power – and having my first baby, that I softened back into being a 'Passionpreneur' – see page 206.)

There is something about Donald Trump's larger-than-life charisma and sense of doing things really BIG which appeals to the (Chinese) Dragon in me. Plus, of course, he is incredibly attractive, in the way that rich, successful, powerful men usually are, and I was dying to meet him at some point in my life.

So of course when I was asked to write this book I saw it as an opportunity to meet Mr Trump in the flesh, and tried in vain to get past the barrage of gatekeepers which guard his kingdom. Normally 'persistence pays', but when you start to feel like a fly round a cow's arsehole it is usually a sign you need to give up – or at least try a different tack.

But I was determined to include Trump in this book, and this chapter is based on his well-documented problems in the early 1990s when the US real estate market crashed. He owed a total of $900million to a total of 99 different banks, and couldn't even afford to service the interest on the loans – let alone repay them. To make matters worse, he had personally guaranteed $100million of the loans, and therefore was facing personal bankruptcy.

The famous story goes that one day, while walking down Fifth Avenue hand in hand with his wife Marla, Trump pointed across the street to a man holding a cup with a guide dog. He asked her 'Do you know who that is?' Maria replied 'Yes, Donald. He's a beggar. Isn't it too bad? He looks so sad!' Trump replied 'You're right. He's a beggar but he's worth about $900million more than me.'

As Trump explains in his book *How To Get Rich* (Random House) when faced with a problem of that size you have two choices: a fearful, defensive one – to give up, curl up and die – or the faithful, riskier one, which is to fight on. Of course, being Donald Trump, and also having not very much to lose at that point, he took the decision to have blind faith that he would resolve the situation, even though the solution was not obvious at the time.

The interesting thing about reading the Trump books is that they are full of messages about positive thinking, about working with high energy and passion towards your goals, and also about having absolute faith and trust in God. These are actually themes which run through every great book on living successfully – from the *Bible* itself, through to *Teachings of the Buddha*, as well as more contemporary titles like Napoleon Hill's *Think and Grow Rich, The Secret* and the brilliant *Ask and It Is Given by* Esther and Jerry Hicks.

I've written more about 'energy' at the end of the book, but once again, Trump's story reinforces the fact that having the right mindset is absolutely *the* crucial determining factor when it comes to the difference between success and failure, both in business and in life.

Soon after the beggar incident, Trump was reminded by his secretary that he had been invited to a black-tie bankers' convention at the Waldorf-Astoria. Attending was actually the last thing he wanted to do – Trump was probably the most hated man in New York at the time, he knew the room would be full of people he owed money to, he was tired and his energy was low. All he wanted to do was go home and watch football on television. So he told his secretary that he would not be going.

But when he got home, he got a second wind and said to himself 'You know what? I think I'll go.' He put on his tuxedo and, as there were no cabs free and he was reluctant to be seen arriving in his chauffeured limo, he walked the 10 blocks to the hotel in the freezing rain. He arrived drenched, feeling at the lowest point in his life.

To make matters worse, he found himself sitting next to someone who refused to acknowledge his presence. After 15 minutes of trying to make conversation to what seemed like a stone wall, Trump discovered that the guy was a notoriously hard-nosed executive who worked for a bank to whom Trump owed $149million, and who had already forced 37 real estate people in New York into bankruptcy.

There were 2,000 people at the convention that night, and it was just Trump's luck to be seated next to one of his archrivals! But Trump saw the opportunity in the adversity – maybe this was more than a coincidence? So he said to the banker, 'You're the one that's killing everybody, and you want to kill me too.' To which the banker replied, 'Yes, we do.'

But Trump continued to make the effort to try to really get to know his enemy. As the evening wore on and the conversation (and wine) started to flow, he found out that the banker was in lots of trouble himself. It might have sounded all-powerful that he had already put 37 people into bankruptcy, but in the banking sector that is an awful lot of debt to write off, not to mention the legal fees involved in so many lawsuits. It also meant that the time spent on chasing 'lost' money was a distraction from new money-making deals. In short, this man was himself actually under acute pressure from his bosses. Losing another $149million would not help matters.

By the end of the evening, Trump had turned his enemy into an ally, simply by being friendly and understanding the view from the other man's position. The following Monday, Trump went to see the banker to renegotiate the terms of his borrowing in a new deal which would give him the time he needed to generate new revenue streams to service the interest, and for the property market to recover.

In the same way, Trump worked his way through all the 99 banks he owed money to, going to see the senior executives personally and inviting them with their respective wives to dinner at his home, assuring them that he would work out a way to repay their loans over time. In the process Trump also became personal friends with many of New York's most influential financial people, and after he had managed his way through the crisis, those same bankers came up with even bigger loans to finance Trump's later deals.

As John Paul Getty once said, 'If you owe the bank $100 that's your problem. If you owe the bank $100million that's the bank's problem.' And at the time, these men were highly receptive to any solution that would see their debts repaid. Although it may not seem like it at the time when you owe huge amounts of money, in many ways, if you are in debt and the debt is large enough, the lender will actually need you more than you need them.

So, as Trump says in his book *Think Big and Kick Ass* (Donald Trump and Bill Zanker, Collins 2007), it actually pays in business to have the vision to do the really big deal – the money is always available if you look hard enough for it, and, if you run into problems down the line, it is actually easier to find a way out of them.

Here are my observations of being in deep problems in business and dealing with a mountain of debt:

- Fear is not a good motivator; it leads you into panic and that makes for bad decision making. Anger and resentment are also emotions which are never far away – and both will alienate all parties if you put them on display. So you need to try to work towards a much more positive mindset – one of hope and optimism – as quickly as possible.

- Even if you are not particularly religious, it helps to call on a 'higher power' to send you the strength to get through your crisis, plus the solutions you need. You need to have absolute faith for this process to work (which actually feels like a deep sense of calm), and almost immediately you will find that new people, opportunities and invitations will start appearing out of the blue. When this happens, keep an open mind and explore everything that comes your way, even though you can't immediately see the logic in doing so at the time.

- Stay positive and see your situation not as a problem but as a challenge which has been sent to strengthen you, and from which you will learn valuable lessons.

- Remember, you are on a life journey, and change is often sent to move you to the next phase of your life, even if it feels uncomfortable at the time. So, even if it all goes pear shaped, bear in mind this could just be life paving the way for something even bigger and better that it has in store for you. Take strength from this extract from Max Ehrmann's famous poem, 'Desiderata':

You are a child of the universe,
no less than the trees and the stars;
you have a right to be here.
And whether or not it is clear to you,
no doubt the universe is unfolding as it should.
Therefore be at peace with God,
whatever you conceive Him to be,
and whatever your labours and aspirations,
in the noisy confusion of life keep peace
with your soul.
With all its sham, drudgery, and broken dreams,
it is still a beautiful world.
Be cheerful.
Strive to be happy.

12

FINDING THE RIGHT BUSINESS

It is all very well battling with competitors and facing mutiny from within your well-established ranks, but many entrepreneurs' initial and perhaps biggest nightmare is the sheer battle of trying to get their concept off the ground.

I've lost count of the number of people who have talked to me about this or that great business idea, but who, when I ask them what they're doing to make their idea a business reality, reply with a list of reasons 'why not'. Lack of capital, their children are too young, they 'don't know how to', they are earning too much money to leave their current job, they're too old, too young – the list of excuses goes on and on! These are the dreamers, the wannabes, the members of the 'coulda-shoulda' club, the ones who sit in pubs and say, 'I had that idea years ago' but who never bothered to actually try to make their business dreams happen.

Probably the biggest nightmare comes when these people are inspired enough to take the plunge, and then the business doesn't immediately take off. The statistics show that something like two-thirds of all business start-ups fail within their first two years, and those that do survive barely manage to keep their heads above water. It's a miserable existence, trying to make ends meet and putting all the hours God sends into a business that is barely keeping its head above water.

Entrepreneurial biographies make it all sound so easy – and looking back, I consider myself extremely lucky to have hit gold with the first idea I chose to act upon. Finding success with your first business idea is incredibly rare. The reality is that many hugely successful entrepreneurs tried their hand (utterly unsuccessfully) at lots of different business ideas before they found the one 'thing' that really clicked and finally worked for them.

The number of businesses which manage to break through the struggle of the early years and actually make it to the big time of becoming a growing, profitable company, with the potential to make their owner a few million pounds, is probably fewer than 5%. Although persistence and determination are key ingredients in entrepreneurial success (see Chapter 13), how do you know if your efforts are finally going to be rewarded with success or whether you are simply banging your head against a brick wall, flogging a business idea that is never going to become anything?

Sometimes it just takes time to find the right business for you.

Laura Tenison MBE, founder of the maternity and babywear business JoJo Maman Bébé, went through a long and agonising business journey before she embarked on launching her maternity-and babywear company which now turns over £18million a year and has already won her a whole clutch of British business awards.

Laura is the perfect example of a person who has the incredible intensity of energy that it takes to be an entrepreneur. I first met her when we were recording Radio 4's *Woman's Hour* in Manchester, just after Red Letter Days had crashed. The topic was how to handle staff (I had just been labelled 'Red Letter Monster' by the *Daily Mail* for the way I had allegedly treated mine) and Laura was there explaining, by contrast, how hers were all just like a big, extended family to her. (Which is also how mine were – that is, before I became 'famous', fell from grace in the media spotlight and they no longer had to 'kowtow' to me so all started trying to sell their stories, dishing the dirt on me, to the tabloid press!)

That was in 2005, and Laura was already a whirlwind of energy, completely outspoken, not a trace of nerves, and with ferociously strong views. By the time I presented her with the Female Entrepreneur of the Year award at the 2007 Fast Growth Business Awards she had become a virtual tornado, bounding up on stage pulsating with vibrant energy and excitement.

One of the cleverest finance directors I ever worked with (although I didn't appreciate him nearly enough at the time), Andy Leeser, always said to me that an entrepreneur was the 'warp core' of a business. Ineffective, unless you create the right setting to capture their energy. (If you're a Trekkie you will know that the 'warp core' was the energy source which powered the Starship

Enterprise.) Likewise, a budding entrepreneur with the right kind of energy to be brilliantly successful in business can be an absolute disaster in most other settings – which is why so many fabulously talented people frequently bomb out of school and manage to get themselves sacked from every job they attempt to hold down.

No experience brought this home to me more than the Ernst & Young International Entrepreneur of the Year Annual Conference and Awards in California in November 2002.

The invitation initially went in the bin (the trip wasn't exactly a freebie), but then I thought – quite correctly as it turned out – 'Maybe this is the only time I'll ever get to be invited'.

I was the only award winner from the UK who bothered to attend, but it was actually one of the best experiences of my life – Virgin Upper Class flights to LA, fabulous 5-star hotel in Palm Springs, brilliant conference speakers including John Bello (founder of the iconic US drinks brand SoBe) and inspirational entrepreneur Pat Croce. The focal point of the event was the US awards gala dinner, hosted by none other than *The Tonight Show* star Jay Leno. Plus, I got to take my new boyfriend along for the trip, so something must have clicked, as he later became my husband.

During our three days in Palm Springs we got to meet all the US award nominees, and I have to say that they were a bunch of the most unemployable maverick oddballs I've ever met. Even though everything in America is larger than life, it made me realise that entrepreneurs really are a different breed to your average person. So, take heart if you've gone through life to date being considered as something of a freak: in business, it could prove to be your biggest asset.

But back to Laura, and here is her story of her struggle to find the right business to start up.

From a young age, Laura had made her own clothes, and this eventually grew into a small-scale clothing business, making clothes for friends. When she left school, she had no idea what she wanted to do with her life, and ended up working for someone else, which she immediately found out didn't suit her.

'I realised that I had this huge amount of energy, and was really intolerant for things being done the wrong way, so I wasn't very good as a junior employee, because I would end up telling everyone in the department what to do. I remember the first company I worked for, called Technical Publishing, which was a division of Dunn & Bradstreet, and I had been brought in to chase advertising in France and Italy because I happen to speak French and Italian.

'I couldn't bear the way the company was run, and I kept telling the managing director exactly what I thought. In the end he said, "Look, what do you want to do?" so I said "I don't think I will ever be happy until I am running the company," to which he replied, "I think you had better go off and work somewhere else."

'He was very sweet; I remember he gave me a lift home afterwards. He was an Italian New Yorker, a very sweet middle-aged man and he told me I just wasn't suited to working with people, because people don't react very well to someone coming into a company and telling everyone else what to do after just two months!

'So I really became self-employed because I wasn't good working for other people. That was quite a big lesson to learn, and after that I decided to set myself up in something to do with clothing manufacturing. I put myself on a self-imposed apprenticeship which consisted of spending 20 months walking around Asia – which is quite a nice thing to do when you're 20. I visited all the silk factories, bought a lot of silk, and worked where I could to earn money. When I came back, I kind of knew what to do with my life, even though I had really done nothing much other than go to school.'

Laura's first aim was to get an apprenticeship in clothing manufacturing, and the plan was then to start her own clothing company, importing fabrics from India or the Far East. 'At that stage I wanted to make an interesting men's wear collection, using ornate silk brocades, a little like English eccentrics or Georgina von Ertstorf.'

She began by writing to clothing manufacturers, telling them she had no experience but was a hard worker. Eventually she landed a job with a small clothes company who gave her the chance of a lifetime and started her at manager level, assisting the buyers. Her hunger to learn increased, and every three months or so she would ask personnel for more responsibility and more work, until she knew the stock room back to front, and was putting her all into her job. The company honoured this and even paid for Laura to learn Japanese (at her request) for an hour a week at a business school nearby. The business-savvy Laura had cottoned on to the rise in Japanese takeovers and had her eye firmly on the future of business.

Within 18 months of this intensive work experience, Laura was ready for a new challenge and was determined to start her own business, but the men's clothes range would have to wait.

'Just by chance, I ended up building houses in France – completely not in the clothing industry at all – but it was purely because I speak fluent French and I'd gone with a friend who wanted to buy a house in France. Her grandmother had left her £10,000 and I went out with her for the weekend and I just couldn't believe how inefficiently everything was done!

'At the time, all the Brits were trying to buy houses in France and you could still buy a cottage for £10,000 or £20,000. So I suddenly thought: "I have to do this". So I went and got someone to teach me how to draw architectural plans and I set up this nice little business, where I would find a derelict cottage, or farm house, and even a couple of chateaux; I'd draw out the plans of what it would look like when it was renovated, and I'd get the renovation costs estimated.

'You would come from Britain, I would pick you up from the airport, and show you six houses which were perfect for British clients, and by the end of the weekend I had almost certainly sold you a house. I had an 80% success rate, it was fantastic. Having been sold the house, you would arrive in rural Brittany and of course, you wouldn't know any local builders, so it became a nice little business, because once I got the customer, they relied on me and we became friends.'

After two years of this, Laura met her husband John, who was based in the UK. Spending most of her time away from John in France and renovating 20 grotty cottages in one go was taking its toll, so she sold her business to the first person who expressed an interest.

Laura was back to square one in her business journey. It is true to say that, in life, sometimes you have to let go of whatever isn't working for you, to make room for the right solution. But things were about to get worse for Laura.

On her way home to the UK Laura was involved in a very bad car crash, breaking 20 bones in her body and being hospitalised for a few weeks. In the bed opposite her was a woman who had been in hospital for ages and had two young girls. One day she expressed her frustration that there was no mail-order company to buy children's clothes from and suggested Laura set one up. Despite her intention to set up a men's clothing range, Laura was inspired.

'I had two broken legs, I was in traction, all my ribs were broken as well as my jaw bone; my eyes were shut and I said to my consultant, "I can't stand it, I have to get out of here, I have a business to set up!" He said, "Laura if you can sit up and get out of bed without fainting, then I will let you go home." So I got up and sat at the end of the bed, and I fainted! But I did end up discharging myself two weeks before they wanted to let me go, which was actually a bad idea because I was still in a huge amount of pain.

A decade on, and JoJo Maman Bébé now has over 250 staff and a turnover of £18million and Laura is franchising the concept across Europe.

As an entrepreneur you may need to try your hand at several businesses, and have some failures, before you find the right business for you. If, in your heart of hearts, you know your current business isn't working, or you're really not enjoying running it, have the courage to let go and try something else.

However, the journey to finding that niche may be long and painful and much of it will be trial and error. Sometimes you won't be sure whether to persevere with what you are doing or to give up on it altogether. Struggling to get started is indeed a business nightmare, so much so that most people never manage to get past 'Go', let alone collect their £200. If you can survive the challenges of this early period and harden yourself to the trials of the business start-up period, you have a much better chance of achieving success later on.

Early business struggles are your trial by fire, and nearly every successful entrepreneur has been forced to endure them.

If you are aching to turn a good idea into a reality and are not sure if it's the right one for you, here's my advice:

- Choose a business that you have a passion for rather than picking a sector just because it will make money. You're going to end up spending 24/7 working on your business, so the biggest gift you can give yourself is to indulge yourself in a hobby or passion that you love. Plus, businesses always work much better when they are run with passion, from the heart.
- Look for inspiration from things you loved doing in your childhood – before your life became polluted by things like money and ambition. Look for lateral ways to combine your interests.
- Don't think you need a never-done-before, new and innovative idea to be a success. There are plenty of businesses out there based on well-established ideas and business models. However, if you do this, the key thing is to choose a much smaller niche of customers and go all out to please them, rather than trying to be all things to all people. The common ground in most sectors is already taken by the big players; that means you need to work around the smaller, more niche, edges.
- By all means look at what your competitors are doing, but the successful small businesses which really break through big time are the ones that capture the customer's attention by being bold enough to do things in a dramatically different way to the status quo. So don't copy – innovate!

13

REJECTION AND RIP-OFFS

I am often asked whether entrepreneurs are born or bred, and my answer is always that, in my view, there are just three key qualities that all successful entrepreneurs possess which make them stand apart from the crowd. Sometimes you are just born with these qualities, but more usually they are built in via a tough childhood. The qualities are:

SELF-BELIEF, DETERMINATION and DRIVE.

If you possess these qualities you absolutely do not need anything else to be successful in business – no capital, no contacts, no experience – and indeed no real talent! All those things can easily be found if you have enough self-belief, determination and drive, because being an entrepreneur is just like being a magician: it is the ability to turn ideas into action, and then assemble all the resources you need to make your business idea a reality. And there is no better story to illustrate the truth of this than that of James Dyson, whose entrepreneurial journey is eloquently explained by the ghostwriter Giles Coren in James's autobiography *Against The Odds* (Textere Publishing 2000). A journey so beset with issues and struggles and adversity it makes incredible reading!

For those of you who have just beamed down from an alien planet, James Dyson is the man who invented the Dyson Dual Cyclone – a product that completely changed the entire vacuum cleaner industry sector, once so dominated by Hoover – and a product which eventually made him a billionaire.

The interesting thing about reading his autobiography is that it is clear that James is a man filled with anger: anger when things don't work properly; anger when people let him down; anger when they betray him; anger when they tell him 'it can't be done'; and anger when they reject him. While I would always advocate that passion is a far better energy source, anger works pretty well too – because it is just another form of highly charged energy which, if channelled in the right way, can be the fuel that propels you towards success.

James was not even a trained engineer and did not have the first clue about how a vacuum cleaner worked. All he had was frustration with the existing product and the knowledge there must be something better.

James had managed to get into the Royal College of Art in the late 1960s, at a time when they were accepting just three students a year who did not have prior degrees. That was the start of his journey of discovery: looking into how things were designed and learning to question whether there was a better way.

It was his frustration while renovating his home that led to his first big invention – the Ballbarrow, created because the wheelbarrow he was using to transport materials across his garden always sank into the mud as he tried to push it along. By simply replacing the wheel with a ball the problem was solved – and because the ball was the key USP of the product, James made it bright orange, so it would stand out as being different and thus naturally attract people's attention.

A brilliant idea, but as always, business is as much about the execution as it is about the invention, and James had real problems trying to get anyone to actually buy the Ballbarrow. His first strategy was to recruit a team of sales women to go out to garden centres and get them to stock the product. A slow-burn process which didn't really work, mainly because the buyers didn't think anyone would want to buy such an odd-looking product.

(Retail buyers are actually often the worst people to sell to; they are frequently employees, not entrepreneurs, and their success is judged by how well their portfolio performs. So, the instant anything new and untested comes along, their immediate instinct is that taking it on would be a risk, which, if the product does not shift, may lose them their job. Hence we still have so many retail shops in the UK filled with drab 'me too' products in safe, boring colours.)

In business it is all too easy to give up when enough people say 'no'. You start to lose confidence in your idea and think that if so many people are saying 'no', then perhaps they must be right. This is where self-belief comes in – with enough self-belief you can still believe you are right and the world is wrong, even if you receive a thousand rejections. It's how many entertainers became famous despite being booed off stage in their early careers.

But it is the second quality – determination – which will propel you towards eventual success. However, the key thing to realise is that determination is NOT about relentlessly pursuing the same approach – it is about subtly changing and trialling until you find the formula that works.

Thus, if James had persisted in trying to sell the Ballbarrow into garden centres via his team of women, a strategy which was clearly not working, eventually he would have run out of money and the business would have folded. Instead, he changed tack and placed a series of tiny little black-and-white classified adverts featuring a line drawing of the Ballbarrow, which asked people to send payment of £19.95. And the cheques started rolling in – all at full retail price (as opposed to selling into garden centres at wholesale price for half that amount), so that his profit margin was effectively tripled.

(Just to explain that arithmetic: typically a retailer will want to make a 50% profit margin. So if the retail price is £20 they will want to buy it for £10. Assume the product costs £5 for you to make it, thus the profit is £5 if you sell into the retailer. However, sell direct to the end customer at £20 and your profit is suddenly £15. So your profit has not doubled, it has tripled. Assuming that it doesn't cost you the earth to market the product yourself (and that is another story), you should in theory be better off by selling direct to the consumer.)

Of course, once a product starts to attract attention at 'grassroots' level, it becomes cult, and once a product becomes cult, suddenly all the retailers want it. Usually going mass market on anything new and innovative is much easier and more successful once you have established a smaller niche market for your product. Enough 'marketing speak' from me, but the book to read on this fascinating subject is *Purple Cow* by Seth Godin, (Penguin Books, 2002) which explains very neatly the life cycle of products – from their adoption by 'innovators' and early users, to the mass market and then to the 'laggards', as demand for the product lapses in favour of something new. Basically, if you can create excitement amongst a small group of fanatics who will tell all their friends, then that is a brilliant (and inexpensive) way to launch anything new. It is a classic viral marketing technique.

So back to James's story. In 1974 the Ballbarrow was taking off, with thousands of direct sales, lots of publicity and even appearances at the Chelsea Flower Show. All of which meant that retailers were clamouring for the product, and also, inevitably, greed started to set in.

James started to make moves to license the product in America and began talks with an American manufacturer called Plascor. Meanwhile, one of his previous employees, a sales manager called John Brannan, flew to the USA with a few samples of the Ballbarrow, and convinced another manufacturer, Glassco, to put a similar product into production. Before James could complete his Plascor deal, Glassco had already brought out a rip-off version, and they had even called it 'Ballbarrow'!

A sobering lesson for all those entrepreneurs out there with their never-been-done-before invention in which they have invested a fortune for patenting. It is one thing having a patent; it is quite another trying to defend it. So James's company, Kirk-Dyson (which he had set up with various backers to manufacture and distribute the product), embarked on a costly legal battle to try to sue Glassco for infringement of their trademark and patents. Meanwhile, back at home, tension was mounting within the Kirk-Dyson board, debts were growing and fear set in.

The company even refused to consider putting any funding into exploring James's latest concept – the Dual Cyclone vacuum cleaner – on the basis that it was a costly whim that would never amount to anything (talk about lack of vision! – see Chapter 16). And amazingly, presumably because they now felt that James was an expensive liability whose work as 'the inventor' was now over, his co-directors turned on James and removed him from the board and from the company (beware the enemies within – see Chapter 9).

There was little James could do but leave. He only had a 33% shareholding in the business and, crucially, he had also allowed the company to register the patent and trademark for Ballbarrow rather than doing so personally. The Ballbarrow continues to sell worldwide to this day, but James will never personally receive a penny from it.

So James learned the hard way: to never again relinquish his rights to any future invention. And the fury at the way he had been treated at Kirk-Dyson was exactly the high-octane rocket fuel that James needed to give him the energy he was going to need to ensure that his next invention – the Dual Cyclone – would be a success.

The journey to create a revolutionary new vacuum cleaner began with James's frustration at using his old Hoover vacuum cleaner, whose performance dropped the moment its bag started to become even a little full. 'Surely there is a way to create a cleaner without a bag?' James thought, and once his mind had been tuned into the problem, the solution appeared in the form of a nearby sawmill, where the sawdust was sucked away by a 30-foot-high cone that spun particles out of the air by centrifugal force.

Inspired and elated, as soon as he got home James ripped the bag off his old Hoover Junior and replaced it with a similar miniature 'cyclone' structure, using just pieces of cardboard gaffer-taped to the machine, and discovered that it could actually work.

That 'eureka moment' happened in October 1978, and with his departure from Kirk-Dyson following hot on its heels in January 1979, James now had the time and space he needed to focus on the invention upon which he would build his fame, his name and his fortune.

It took five years and 5,127 prototypes to finally get the Dual Cyclone into mainstream production and distribution – and it was James's absolute belief in his product, combined with sheer persistence and determination, which enabled him to succeed where many others would have inevitably given up along the way.

But the most amazing thing about James's story is the sheer brick wall of resistance from seemingly every quarter, sonegative towards him and his product during that five-year journey. It started with one of the directors on the board of Kirk-Dyson refusing to provide the investment he needed to create a prototype, saying, 'But

James, your idea can't be any good. If there were a better kind of vacuum cleaner, Hoover or Electrolux would have invented it.' So, using £25,000 that he scraped together, plus £25,000 which he persuaded a friend to invest in the business, James, decided to go it alone.

It took three long years of making prototype after prototype in his workshop at home, with no money coming in and a mortgage mounting, for James to perfect his new vacuum cleaner. By now, with debts of £79,000, James had no alternative but to go out and start trying to make some money by licensing the idea to a manufacturer.

His first approach was to Hoover, who tried to make him sign an agreement prior to meeting according to, which, as the small print revealed, that anything that came out of discussions would be owned by Hoover itself. James declined. Then, over the next two years, James approached every manufacturer you could think of.

Hotpoint told him the idea was 'dead from the neck up'; Electrolux told him he would 'never sell a cleaner without a bag'; AEG tried to make the machine suck up a huge pile of rubbish and then claimed it didn't work; Goblin refused to see him because they were on a two-day week because their sales were so low and 'no one had time'. James endured rejection after rejection over a two-year period while his debts continued to mount and his hope of success looked extremely bleak.

In desperation, and despite having been burned by his experience with Ballbarrow, James went to the USA to see if he could find a manufacturer and a market there. But he was to find a different kind of disappointment –

lots of positive meetings and talk which raised his hopes, only for them to be dashed by lack of follow-through or a last-minute failure to complete. To put it into Essex speak, America was all mouth and no trousers. But James did experience a small breakthrough by managing to get Zanussi to manufacture 500 machines that were sold via the home shopping brand Kleeneze.

Finally, in April 1984, after knocking on every door imaginable, James was offered a deal by the American giant Amway, who wanted to license the Dual Cyclone in return for a huge sum, which would sort all of his mounting financial problems. So James flew out with his business partner Jeremy Fry to sign the deal. But to his blank astonishment he was told the deal had changed to a new, lower amount. Despite this, desperate for money, he accepted the revised deal and flew back to the UK relieved and elated.

More misery was about to come, as later that year he received a letter from Amway's solicitors accusing him of fraudulent conduct, deception and misrepresentation, on the basis that the invention was not ready for market. Once again he was plunged into expensive litigation, this time with a multi-billion-dollar US giant. After months of litigation, James finally settled with Amway – but only on the basis that he had to repay the money they had advanced him. Once again he was broke, depressed, and back to square one.

But then followed a stroke of good fortune. The Cyclon, as it was originally called, had been featured in an American design annual, which generated just one single request for information – from Japan. So James, despite having literally no money, flew East on the cheapest Aeroflot flight available via Moscow, in a last-ditch attempt to make something of his invention.

The Japanese company, Apex, thought the machine was wonderful. They understood exactly what James was trying to do and also how to sell it. Within three weeks they had signed a deal with James that gave him an advance on royalties and thus some much-needed cash.

James spent much of that following year in Japan, working with Apex's team to get the manufacturing processes right. The cleaner had to be renamed the G-Force due to various trademark issues, and was eventually launched in March 1986. It was lavender and pink and ridiculously expensive at £1,200 per machine, but like the Ballbarrow before it, it was exactly those 'Purple Cow' attributes that grabbed attention, and the G-Force soon became the 'must have' domestic item in Tokyo. It took a while for sales to build, but within three years G-Force was making sales of £12 million a year.

But James himself didn't see any of the money, and once again embarked on a battle, this time with Apex, to extract the royalties he believed he was owed. Eventually James sold off the Japanese rights altogether, knowing that the money he would gain plus the momentum he had already established would now enable him to take the product mass-market in the West.

Once again to America, and in another twist of fate James found himself on a flight sitting next to a businessman who was reading the same Fay Weldon novel. They got talking and James discovered he ran a Canadian manufacturing company called Iona, who subsequently agreed to take the G-Force on and market it across North America.

Just when James thought he had made another breakthrough, a call came through from Chicago to say there was a problem. Amway had just launched an identical machine, in breach of at least four of James's patents. So another lawsuit began! But this time, James actually had some money to fight it with.

Meanwhile, his invention – a success in Japan and the USA – started to attract attention from the UK, and in 1991 James got a call from Vax asking if he could build them an upright vacuum cleaner for the UK market. Once again the project launched with great gusto, but problems emerged and James eventually came to the realisation that if he was ever going to get his vacuum cleaner into production in the UK he would simply have to do it himself. So he once again risked all the cash he had made, as well as raising finance to create a UK manufacturing operation.

Finally, on 1 July 1993, the first Dual Cyclone came off the production line – 15 years on from that day in 1978 when he had first had the seed of his idea. A machine built by his own staff in his own factory; a machine that was destined to change the entire domestic appliance sector. Unsurprisingly, all those detractors who had refused to help James in his early years started to copy the Dual Cyclone, including Hoover, whom in 1999 James gleefully and successfully sued for patent infringement. There are now 18 types of James's cleaner on the market and the company has around a 40% market share – not bad for a machine which no one would touch a decade earlier.

James's phenomenal success is a real testimony to the value of persistence and determination when you know deep in your heart that you have the most fantastic product, that is superior to everything else on the market. If you are reading this as an entrepreneur just starting out and struggling to get your business off the ground, experiencing rejection after rejection, sinking ever deeper into debt while the world is mocking your efforts, I urge you to get hold of James Dyson's autobiography. It may just give you the strength to carry on.

Remember, the darkest hour is often just before the dawn.

Here are a few observations about persistence in the face of rejection:

- Read any successful person's life story and you will soon realise that every single one of them – whether entrepreneurs or entertainers – endured many years of relentless rejection and humiliation before they finally found success. Think of it as the apprenticeship you need to serve if you want to succeed in business.

- Persistence is not just about relentlessly plugging away at something in the same way day after day, year after year. You need to trial every single way and approach that you can think of to find your breakthrough.

- I wrote in Chapter 12 that if you are struggling with a go-no-where business it could make sense to focus on something else. But if the business you are currently struggling with is truly 'The One', then you will know deep in your heart that it is right to keep fighting on.

- Overnight success is extremely rare – success usually builds over time.

- Once you reach a tipping point, that is, when the offers, opportunities and cash really start to pour in, this is the glorious point at which you achieve 'momentum' in business – and everything can start to flow very fast and furiously. Momentum is very difficult to achieve – and is worth a huge amount of money precisely for that reason.

14

GOING INTO BUSINESS WITH FAMILY AND FRIENDS

One of the great things that came out of the crash of Red Letter Days was that it gave me the freedom to move out of London and the South-East. My husband is from Yorkshire and although I didn't want to move that far North, we found a fabulous private school in the Peak District which could accommodate all three of our school-age boys, and so we relocated to Bakewell in April 2006.

I thought our move to the area had been pretty low key, but within days of our arrival the Indian takeaway home-delivery man was asking my husband, 'Is it true a celebrity now lives here?' About a week after we had moved in, I had a surprise visit from our nearby 'next door neighbour' (by rural standards!), the founder and chief executive of the training company A4e, and star of

Channel 4's *Make me a Million*, Emma Harrison, who left a note saying, 'Pop over for tea sometime'. News travels fast.

I'd only met Emma twice before: fleetingly at the Ernst & Young Entrepreneurial Masterclass in London in 2003 (we had both won an Ernst & Young Entrepreneur of the Year Award the previous year), and later in 2005 when we were doing *Woman's Hour* on Radio 4 together.

I did eventually pop round for tea, and quickly realised, as I was halfway up the magnificent driveway, that she lived in a 20-bedroom stately home – worth 10 times as much as my own new humble abode!

Emma's story is a famous one.

After she left university at the age of 23 her dad invited her into his small Sheffield-based training business (which specialised in getting unemployed steel workers back into jobs), to give her some work experience. Only 18 days later he told her she'd got the hang of it, and promptly disappeared to Germany leaving her in charge.

Within a year she'd taken turnover from £100,000 to £1million, simply by speaking to people in government departments about their issues – and undertaking to solve them. By the time she was 28, turnover had hit £3million, but the business was stalling.

After many tough and penniless years, Emma's father and two brothers were now enjoying the fruits of her labours and constantly draining the company's bank account to fuel their own luxury lifestyle that included motor cruising in the Mediterranean.

'My dad's personality began to change. He would call and threaten me; accusing me of moving money around bank accounts. He told me he would sack me and get someone better; his personality went from that of a genuine loving, brilliant man to one of complete paranoia. When I said I couldn't do it anymore, he would tell me I was the goose that laid the golden egg and that I wasn't going anywhere.

'Despite not having been involved in the business for years, he became a control freak and told me I couldn't run the business without him. I started to suffer a serious lack of confidence. I would work all day and go home and sit on my bed and cry all night. My father would constantly write cheques against the company to fund his "life of Riley" while I was slaving away to earn the cash. One December, Dad took £500,000 from the company's bank account and wiped out the money I needed to pay the staff salaries. So I had to go and see him to beg for some funds – it was Christmas and people needed to be paid.'

What Emma didn't realise until later was that her dad's behaviour was actually the onset of Parkinson's disease.

At about this time, Emma met Jim Harrison (who later became her husband), who was running his family's business – and saw just how a normal, healthy, family business relationship could work. 'I realised I was in a dysfunctional business and just how unhappy I was. I realised I would rather walk away than continue. But I had learned from my dad to think and plan ahead. Because my father would not even discuss the issues by this point, I wrote him a letter stating that six months from that date I would resign and that everything I had created would be his.'

Exactly six months later, she did.

Emma walked away from the business and told her father that every single penny and asset within the business was his to do with as he wanted. Then, using all the contacts and experience she had gained, along with all the loyal staff who followed her from the old business, she created a new company, Action for Employment (A4e), which remains under her total control to this day.

Suddenly, with all the baggage of family feuds behind her and no one to control or question her, she was finally free to accelerate momentum and drive the business forward.

'I gathered my senior team together and painted my vision of a company whose mission was to improve people's lives. I told them our strategy would be to expand through increasing the scope of the services we offered, as well as the geography – we were only operating in five cities at that time and I wanted to be in 20.

'We had contracts worth £3million and I told them we would drive them to £10million in year one, consolidate to £15million in year two, and then double growth to £30million in year three. While I had a great team, they nearly fell on the floor laughing! But then, no one had laughed in that business for at least a year, and we were now finally free to reinvent the business. In inspiring the team, I opened their thinking and I had also removed all the barriers. In the end they delivered £12million, £17million and £35million.'

It's 14 years on, and A4e is now turning over £100 million and is the prime contractor to the government. In addition it manages £250million in government funds. The business now has 1,850 employees and the number is increasing all the time. The geography now extends internationally to countries including Israel and Poland and Emma's mission is to increase turnover to £500 million by 2014.

Incredible achievements, which only came about once the basic structure of the business was put onto a proper and professional footing. Sadly, Emma's father has since died, but I am sure he passed away immensely proud of his daughter's magnificent success. Emma's nightmare is actually a classic one.

I made exactly the same kind of mistake as Emma by starting Red Letter Days in partnership with my brother's girlfriend, Sabina. It just seemed far safer that way. Sabina was not working and was keen to get involved in something; I was freelancing in accountancy to make ends meet, and so didn't have the time to devote to manning an office full time. Joining forces seemed like the natural solution: we were both eager to start something new, and got on really well as friends.

At the start, we toured the country together, visiting all the 'experience suppliers' whom we would eventually feature in our first brochure by day, and retiring to the local curry house by night, charged with enthusiasm, in the mood to celebrate and to discuss our future plans. But when people go into business (and we were no exception) they often think it is a one-way street to overnight riches and success and that once you turn on the tap money will just start pouring out. Of course, it never works like that.

Putting all your suppliers and administration in place is the easy bit; actually getting the business to generate revenue is the difficult challenge where most businesses fail.

After a disastrous first Christmas – when we took just a handful of orders despite having blown something like £25,000 (of MY money!) on advertising that just didn't work, it was difficult to see how the business could survive. My business partner quickly lost interest when she realised it wasn't Easy Street and that she definitely wouldn't be becoming an overnight millionaire. Much to my annoyance, she would frequently leave the office telephones on answering machine, so whatever small amount of interest we managed to generate was quickly lost. Relations became very strained indeed.

Eventually I took the decision that I had to move everything from our office in Chelmsford to my home in London, where it could be under my control, and my mum intervened to buy Sabina out for £1,000 (even though she hadn't paid for her initial shares in the first place, and her stake was technically worthless – plus I really felt she had let the side down and didn't actually deserve a penny). But it seemed a small price to pay to avoid a family war (my brother later married her, although they are now divorced), and mum later transferred the shares back to me as a gift.

It was probably a good 10 years before I really got back on speaking terms with my ex-partner again – by which time Red Letter Days was turning over several million a year and starting to make really good profits.

These kind of start-up partnership horror stories, whether families or not, are also echoed in many of the emails I receive from people struggling to make their own businesses work.

The biggest problem with internal struggles is that they hugely detract your energy from the real issues you should be focusing on: driving your business forward, doing deals, making sales, getting cash flowing! As the business stalls, more and more time is spent blaming each other than actually getting things done. Eventually the situation becomes untenable and the business inevitably implodes.

When family are involved, this can also destroy relationships. One woman I was trying to help confided in me that she would fight like cat and dog with her business-partner husband after every business crisis, to the point where he would become physically violent and drag her round the room by her hair. Finally they separated and the business is no more. When business affects your family relationships you have to ask yourself whether it is worth it.

It is also worth considering the fact that investors are particularly allergic to investing in husband-and-wife partnerships – quite simply because the risk of failure is so much higher than with partnerships based on normal commercial relationships.

Consider the most successful entrepreneurs for a moment; the vast majority achieved it on their own. Yes, they had helpers and strong people behind the scenes, but generally the main driving force behind the business came from just one person, who was absolutely determined and focused on making the business work.

So while it seems like a much safer and far more comfortable option to go into business with family and friends – or even colleagues whom you perhaps used to work with – be very careful indeed that you are absolutely prepared for what you are letting yourself in for.

Here are my thoughts on going into business partnerships with others:

- If you are thinking of going into business with family and friends, be ruthlessly honest with yourself about the reasons why. What unique skills or other input (eg investment) will they bring to the table? Crucially, ask yourself, whether you would employ these people if they came to you for interview. If any part of the reason behind your decision is to shore up your self-esteem or to make things feel 'safer', then you are almost certainly storing up problems for the future.
- Sit down and discuss in detail exactly what role each of you will play in the business and where your individual responsibilities will lie, including how much time you are each prepared to commit to the business. Also ensure that you discuss the disaster scenario of how you will unravel the partnership if things do not work out – whether by amicable exit or if any one party wishes to force closure. This isn't being negative, it's being pragmatic.
- Document everything, preferably in a legally binding document. But if you don't have the money to spend on legal fees, even a simply worded letter of agreement jointly constructed and signed by all parties is better than nothing. Although it seems like a waste of time for a start-up business with no revenue, you should also have basic service and shareholder agreements drawn up (if you are a limited company) or a partnership agreement (if you are entering into this as a partnership). Crucially, bear in mind that partnerships usually involve unlimited liability, meaning you could personally become responsible for any debts run up by your partner – even if you're not aware of them. Creating a limited company is usually a far better route.

- Be very, very careful to ensure that signing authorities for all the business bank accounts prevent any one party extracting money from the business without the other's knowledge. Ensure you also have a proper process in place to control purchase authorities and, crucially, joint signing authority over any contracts the company/partnership enters into. One mistake or piece of bad judgement in this area can easily bring an entire business down.
- Better than all the above, just do it on your own!

15

GIVING BAD CREDIT

One of my fellow Dragons, Peter Jones, told me about his biggest nightmare when we went out for a drink together one day after one of the filming sessions for the first series of *Dragons' Den*. At the time, problems were emerging with my Red Letter Days business and Peter's intervention at that stage gave the company a lifeline and valuable breathing space that helped it survive to fight another day. I think he shared his experiences with me to make me feel better about the struggles I was going through with my business. Peter's nightmare resulted from a simple error of assumption.

Peter originally started out in business at the age of 16, when he founded a tennis coaching academy, simply because he had a passion for both business and sport. By the mid-1980s, when computers were just bursting onto the scene, Peter (who was twenty-something and highly ambitious) saw an opportunity to make far more money in IT than in tennis.

He set up a computer company supplying computer equipment and software and was soon riding high on the technology wave, with all the trappings of a successful entrepreneur: a luxury home, a BMW and Porsche in the garage, and a wife with two children. But in his late twenties, disaster struck.

Peter had several clients, mostly well-known corporate companies. He supplied a lot of these companies on credit, with one company in particular ordering a few hundred thousand pounds worth of equipment and support. That is the kind of deal that doesn't come along in business often and for the average entrepreneur it's a chance to make the kind of profit that most people don't earn in an entire year. Plus a successful deal with a blue-chip company, handled efficiently, has the potential to lead to many more future orders. Crucially, Peter didn't run a check on the company.

So the deal was done, the equipment was delivered, and a few days later, day Peter decided to make a courtesy visit to his new client to check that they were happy with the service provided. But when he arrived at the company's offices he was told that the company was in the hands of receivers. He was told to detail any claim he might have, send in writing, and they would look at it shortly. The offices didn't seem to have much furniture left and, seemingly, also had no staff. More importantly, Peter couldn't see any sign of the computer equipment delivered and installed by his company.

Peter had been given the option several months earlier to take out credit insurance for less than £12,000 per annum but decided not to and save the money. This decision cost Peter his business, because, within months of this company going out of business, so did a couple of others, owing him thousands.

Peter's business just couldn't survive that kind of loss and so he was forced to put his company into voluntary liquidation. The financial meltdown impacted on him personally and the pressure ended his marriage, which collapsed acrimoniously soon afterwards.

So, at the age of 28, Peter found himself penniless and living in a vacant office, while he got himself back on his feet. There was no furniture so he slept on a mattress the floor, and no shower – just a hand basin with cold running water to wash in. Peter lived that way for six months apart from a couple of weeks when he stayed with his parents.

With no capital and no asset base, Peter was forced to take a salaried job to make ends meet. That job was with the electronics giant Siemens in their PC division. Within a year he was running the subsidiary.

From there, Peter went to work for the entrepreneur John Caudwell as his managing director running his distribution business 20:20 Logistics. In 1998 after a successful 12 months and having got his finances back in some kind of order, he decided, with savings of £10,000, to start a distribution company that would package and exclusively sell Ericsson mobile phones to major mobile phone retailers and networks.

Once again, riding on the crest of a booming new industry wave, the company grew phenomenally, from nothing to a turnover of £186million just six years later, generating annual net profits of over £5million.

Peter now has a girlfriend and three more children and, ironically, is significantly better off than he was when running that first computer business.

The mobile phone sector continues to be buoyant mainly now due to people wanting the latest new phone that comes out, but Peter has, over the last few years, invested in other business segments. He now has a very diverse portfolio of businesses. He now has a TV production company, various *Dragons' Den* investment businesses, not to mention the 50% stake he acquired in Red Letter Days when he teamed up with Theo Paphitis to buy it out of administration in 2005.

Today, on his website, Peter declares, 'I don't have a fear of failure because for me I class failure as feedback. I think if you fail, the thing to do is to learn from it. We can see so many very successful people who have failed so many different times. I have failed myself and I know what it's like but I think you take that and you learn from it. I think my smartest business move was not to give up – because there have been times for me when I've created a business and things have not gone well for me and I could have quite easily have said "I can't do this, I've given up".'

Actually, if you want to be philosophical about it, you could say that Peter's failure at the age of 28 was one of the best things that ever happened to him. Without that failure he would not have been set on the new path which led him to his current wealth – as well as his TV fame. But it's difficult to be philosophical when you are going through business meltdown and you have just lost everything.

To avoid the pain of a business meltdown, make sure you check all the business details – because assumption is the mother of all f*ck ups in business.

My top tips on the perils and powers of assumption in business, and doing major deals:

- In business the devil is in the detail – check, check and re-check again. Don't delegate your responsibility for the detail in any key area of your business.
- The settlement terms are often just as important to the negotiation as the price you finally agree for the deal. Negotiate long settlement terms with your suppliers but insist on cash on delivery from your customers. Structuring deals in this way can add several per cent to the margin you can earn (money in the bank has a value), as well as de-risking the deal.
- If you decide to give credit to a customer as an incentive for them to do the deal (or alternatively if they refuse to do the deal without it), always undertake a Dun & Bradstreet credit check on the company. It's not complicated or expensive, but it could save you your business.
- Do not be seduced into thinking that a company called a 'plc' must be big and established – any company can call itself a 'plc' provided it has £50,000 of share capital, and contrary to popular misconception, it does not need to be listed on the Stock Exchange.
- Use the power of assumption to your own advantage – when you are small and just starting out, if you look and act like a big company, the majority of people will assume you are. There are lots of devices available to the small company to give it the aura of being large – virtual offices, telephone answering services, even upgrading your own company's status to that of plc.

16

NOT EVERYONE WILL SHARE YOUR VISION

No book on business nightmares written by me could be complete without at least one chapter expounding my views on the British banking system. Since the meltdown of Red Letter Days (which was forced into administration after our bank bonded over £3million of our cash reserves), many entrepreneurs have shared with me their own horror stories of how their bank has played a part in their business downfall, whether through refusing to support when times got tough or pulling the plug on them at the first sign of problems.

The thing that leaves the bitterest taste in the mouth is that the spoils of business meltdown – when companies are plucked out of administration for peanuts or large fees extracted by so-called 'corporate-turnaround specialists' – frequently go on a nod and a wink to those people who are within the banks' close circle of contacts, not to the entrepreneur who created the business, nor the shareholders who invested in it, nor indeed the creditors of the company. In Red Letter Days' case, the £3million cash was withheld on the basis that this was the amount of money that would be required to fulfil the experience vouchers which had been purchased by credit card, should the company go tits up. In addition, there was £1.25million of other security – including £500,000 of personal guarantees from myself and my co-director (mine secured on my home) plus an 'insurance bond', sold to us at a huge premium by (yes, you've guessed it) our bank. But despite pleading with the bank to release these bonded monies back to us (our then chairman Sir Rodney Walker even wrote a letter to the bank's CEO), they would not relent.

A year after the company was pushed through administration, it transpired that the underlying cost of fulfilling the vouchers concerned was £1.5million – meaning that the company was 'over-bonded' to the tune of almost £3million. Had the company had the use of that cash, it could have traded through its difficulties, obtained the pre-IPO funding it needed (where investors buy shares in anticipation of the company floating on the stock market, in the hope that its share price will increase) and floated on AIM as planned in the spring of 2006.

To add insult to injury, the bank awarded the entire £3million of cash reserves to the people who bought the company out of administration (who paid just £250,000 for it) and so not a penny of the over-bonded monies went to the creditors of the company, despite the fact that the profit from those sales had been generated while they were stakeholders. The remaining balance of cash at the bank (*c.* £300,000) was sucked up in its entirety by the fees of the administrators.

In the aftermath of the Red Letter Days meltdown, I actually took legal advice as I was convinced that our bank had acted illegally – not only in bonding the monies unlawfully but also in paying them across to the new owners. But my lawyer just said to me, 'Rachel, do you want to spend all your money plus the next five years fighting a bank, or do you just want to drop it and move on with your life?'

Of course he was right. But that doesn't stop me talking about it at every business event I now speak at! Not only do I want the bank to pay for their actions one way or another – but hell hath no fury like an entrepreneur burned.

But my experience with our bank does illustrate that entrepreneurs are to bankers what chalk is to cheese; they are diametrically opposed in almost every respect. Small-minded, risk-averse pessimists as opposed to visionary, optimistic gamblers. My newborn son has a cute zoo-print outfit which says on it 'Rhinos and Lilos do not mix' – and that line pretty much sums up the relationship when entrepreneurs and banks come together to work in business. Although, to be fair, we saw from the Nothern Rock calamity what can result when an entrepreneur is put in charge of running a bank.

Almost every entrepreneur I interviewed for this book had a horror story to tell me about their dealings with a bank at some point in their business career. I believe there is a reluctance on the part of our banking system to support great British businesses, and no entrepreneurial story highlights this better than that of Lord Karan Bilimoria CBE, the creator of Cobra Beer.

Karan started out in business at the age of 26 with nothing to his name except a £20,000 student debt (he did have a law degree from Cambridge and a chartered accountancy qualification – though it's questionable whether those are a help or a hindrance when you have the ambition to become an entrepreneur!).

'We really roughed it. I was helping a friend of mine and had nowhere to live so he gave me a room in his house. It had no curtains and no bed, just a mattress on the floor. So I went out and bought a chest of drawers and the bottom drawer became my first filing cabinet. My partner in the business was still working for a commodities broker in the City; we were starting to import things like polo sticks from India and I used the kitchen table to work from, making the sales calls.

'After six months we decided that if we wanted to make our business work we would really have to throw ourselves into it. My partner and I moved into a flat on the Fulham Palace Road (London); we each had a bedroom and there was a big sitting/ dining room at the top of the house which we used as our office. By this point we were starting to import beer, and crates of bottles would be delivered, which we would carry up the stairs to that room.'

The business grew organically in the beginning. Karan had found a niche market, selling his imported beer to Indian restaurants because it particularly complemented Indian food. He soon realised he would need to perfect the formula for European tastes and moved to brewing his own Cobra brand in the UK. He relentlessly developed and enhanced the brewing process to the point where Cobra was the number one beer of choice in Indian restaurants throughout the UK. He had cleverly cornered a very lucrative niche market, in a sector that was incredibly competitive and saturated with mainstream beer brands.

But success brings its own challenges, and demand for Cobra grew to such an extent that the business had to dramatically expand. And that needed finance. Using his accountants as his advisors, Karan initiated a share issue to raise £500,000 in a deal which valued the company at £2million. Investors were in place and the legal process was under way – but cash was also running out and it was the company's busiest time of year.

'The bank called and said that we were over our overdraft limit and that they would refuse to honour any further payments on our account. This was despite knowing that the share issue process was well under way; in fact the accountants had by that point already received cheques from investors totalling £50,000.

'I spoke to our bank manager but he was unrelenting. I told him that if you cannot believe a reputable accountancy firm and if you cannot believe me, with my integrity, my qualifications and my reputation, then that means no trust is there. I told him that he could be sure that as soon as the share issue was completed I would move banks. So we struggled through and of course after the deal I moved straight away.

'I often think of that individual bank manager; with such an ugly, blinkered attitude, I often wonder what happened to him.

'I haven't got anything against that bank as such, just that one individual who behaved to us in a certain way. It took me a long time in business to realise that when we start out, we expect the banks to be there to help. In reality banks are not risk takers, that is not their job, and the reward they take is not a high-risk return. The margin they make on lending is small – they are not venture capitalists – and in their business model they cannot afford to make more than a certain number of errors. So by nature they have to be more cautious.

'There is no question that banks are invariably in a very powerful position, because they are the lenders with the security, but I don't think banks abuse that. It's just that the individuals in the banks frequently make their decisions without taking into account the commercial reality of the situation, or using their judgement and trust in the individual running it.'

Karan's second banking experience happened two years later, in 1999. The company had come through a lot of problems after it had been boycotted by part of the Indian restaurant trade, and while the business was back on track, it needed to increase its overdraft facility. 'I had been introduced to a new banking contact via our accountants and went to meet with this quite senior guy at the bank's head office in the City.

'This chap said in a very arrogant way, "I am not going to take your business on. It's going to be more trouble than it's worth. I don't believe any of your valuations and we are not going to give you the facility you are asking for." At this stage the accountants had valued the business at £4million and the bank manager just said, "If your valuation proves to be anywhere near that, I will eat my hat."'

The story had an amusing end a couple of years later when the brand had really taken off. By then Cobra was in all the supermarkets with a massive distribution and Karan was winning awards for his business. 'I was at a lunch at the London Chamber of Commerce and the seat next to me was vacant but I recognised from the place name that it was the same bank manager. When the chap finally arrived, I turned round and said, "Oh it's you!", and of course he recognised me immediately. I said, "Why, I am so disappointed that you are not wearing a hat." To which he replied, "What are you talking about?" I said, "Well, I was looking forward to you eating it."'

Cobra is now an international brand with a turnover of about £100million – by any bank's standards, an extremely valuable corporate client to have. But of course, not all banks are visionary enough to spot a potential goldmine. If an award-winning, high-flying entrepreneur, with a Cambridge law degree, chartered accountancy qualification (and now a member of the House of Lords to boot) can't manage to pull in banking support when it's needed, what hope is there for the rest of us?

Of course, it's not just bankers who will fail to share your vision. Your entrepreneurial journey will be littered with small-minded people who just don't see what you see – be they investors, retail buyers, staff within your company, even your friends and family. You can't waste your energy getting angry with these people, because if they did share your vision, they would be entrepreneurs too, and not working in some dead-end job in someone else's company. Entrepreneurs are by definition different to the crowd and, in this respect, in business you are often 'on your own'.

For what it's worth (from someone whose business journey has been plagued with disastrous banking relationships – so a bit like taking marriage guidance advice from Elizabeth Taylor), here are my top tips for dealing with banks:

- Easier said than done for the average optimistic entrepreneur, but, when putting together financial forecasts, try to under-promise. This will allow you to over-deliver later – and earn a lot of brownie points.
- Don't expect banks to take on risk. It's not in their nature. Think what collateral you have to offer and bear in mind that refusal to take on personal guarantees is often a sign to banks that you don't 100% believe in your business. If you don't believe in your business, then why should they?
- Overdrawn positions can be sustained for a very long time – provided receipts continue to flow at a stable rate. It's when receipts dry up that you have a problem.
- Bank managers (and the credit committees that sit behind them) are frequently egotistical people who possess small pockets of power. Don't antagonise or belittle them or they may be tempted to use that power against you. You catch more bees with honey. (Even as I was writing this chapter, it was in the clear knowledge that some banker, somewhere, some day, is going to delight in making me live to regret it.)
- Avoid all emotion (especially if you are a woman) – from anger to tears and everything in between. Banks like to deal with people who are in control (or at least, who appear to be).

- In times of business trouble it's tempting to hide your problems. Don't. Keep the bank appraised of any issues well in advance – they don't like shocks and surprises.
- If your relationship with your bank is becoming untenable, expect the process of changing banks to take at least three months. Act sooner rather than later.

17

RUNNING OUT OF TIME

Sir James Goldsmith, who died in 1997, was one of the world's most flamboyant billionaires. Father to Jemima and Zac, both now high profile in their own right, and husband to Lady Annabel, after whom the famous London nightclub Annabel's was named, he made the bulk of his fortune in the 1960s and 1970s through the ruthless takeover and asset-stripping of companies which had lost their way, including Bovril and the Grand Union chain in the USA. While other corporate raids proved unsuccessful, they still made him money, including his attempted acquisition of the tyre manufacturer Goodyear, which netted him a profit of $93million. (When you mount a 'corporate raid' you start to buy up shares on the stock market in a company you consider to be undervalued. Of course as soon as word gets out that the company is subject to a take-over bid, the share price rockets. Even if the bid fails, often the share price settles at a higher price than before, leaving the raider sitting on a nice profit.) Yet his success may have not been possible had Sir James not narrowly avoided bankruptcy in the 1950s.

James (or Jimmy) Goldsmith was born in France in 1933 into the wealthy Goldschmidt family of merchant bankers. Sent to be educated at Eton by his millionaire father, Goldsmith rebelled, leaving at the age of 16, to become something of a playboy before his father bailed him out of his gambling debts in return for his agreeing to join the Royal Artillery.

Goldsmith first hit the newspaper headlines when he eloped with the 18-year-old daughter of a Bolivian tin magnate (much to her father's annoyance), but tragically his young wife died of a brain haemorrhage while pregnant with their first daughter, Isabel. The baby was delivered prematurely by caesarean section, and James was left as a single father determined to make his fortune to provide stability for his daughter.

His brother Teddy had started a small pharmaceutical business in Paris, Laboratoires Cassene, and Goldsmith decided to use this business as the basis for his new empire while his brother was away on military service. He started acquiring the rights from big US pharmaceutical manufacturers to distribute their products in France – brands like Alka-Seltzer and Vick Inhalant. He also saw a gap in the market for lower-cost, higher-margin generic versions of the top-selling medicines and persuaded the pharmaceutical wholesalers to agree to allow him to supply them. By the time Teddy returned from the military, the company had over 100 staff and a turnover of £1.5million.

But the business was undercapitalised, expanding too fast, and Goldsmith was heading for bankruptcy. He knew he would need to take emergency action, and negotiated a deal to sell 50% of his business to an Italian company who would provide the injection of cash he so desperately needed.

Using the classic 'delaying tactics' business trick, the Italians dragged the process out, asking for more and more information, knowing that with every day Goldsmith would be becoming more and more desperate to complete on the deal. Finally, at the 11th hour, they agreed to complete, but on the basis that they would take 80% of the business.

In his book *Tycoon: The Life of James Goldsmith* (Grafton, 1988) Geoffrey Wansell records Goldsmith's reaction:

'Well, there's no deal then,' he told them in a fury.

'But you're going to go bust in about three weeks!' they said.

'I can imagine circumstances,' Goldsmith told them fiercely, 'when a man who was much in love with a beautiful mistress, would rather see her dead than in the arms of someone else.' And he ushered the dazed Italians to the door.

'That is exactly what I said and exactly what I felt,' he remembers, 'because I really loved that business. I loved it as much as you could possibly love a business. I had created every brick. I'd built it, recruited everybody, designed every pack, every bit of advertising, everything.' Sir James, I cannot tell you how much I identify with your words.

Time was now running out, and another deal had to be found within a matter of days if Goldsmith was to avoid bankruptcy.

A despondent Jimmy Goldsmith looked around to see if he could find anyone else to help. 'I tried desperately to borrow money. My life was split between bankers, trying to raise money; and creditors, trying to stave them off. Some of our suppliers were so worried that they started to visit me.

'On Sunday 9 July 1957 I realised I had failed. Bills of exchange, which I did not have the money to honour, were due to be presented at the bank the following day and I expected to be declared a bankrupt at once. That was a great deal more serious in France than many people realised. It meant the end of a man's career. It was impossible to recover from it. At that time the dishonour was enormous.'

Yet a strike by bank staff, the first in France for 20 years, saved him from ruin. It gave him the precious time he needed to corral another deal with the French pharmaceutical giant Laboratoires Roussell. He ended up selling the company outright to them, but received £120,000 as part of the deal – enough money to allow Goldsmith to establish the other business ventures upon which he would eventually build his fortune.

Goldsmith's story has great resonance with me, when I think back to the morning of 1 August 2005: 'crunch time' for Red Letter Days' future. It was a Monday, and the previous day the Sunday newspapers had been full of speculation that Red Letter Days was about to crash. We were at a meeting with the lawyers DLA, who were handling the legals on behalf of our proposed administrators. Hope was fading fast, and I was ground down and physically exhausted: I had my week-old baby with me, and was trying to breastfeed in between discussions.

(Like Jimmy Goldsmith, we had had a deal fall through on us at the 11th hour from a company whose chairman (who I think fancied himself as something of a modern-day Julius Caesar) placed the blame on a pot of yoghurt called 'Rachel's Organic Forbidden Fruit' that his wife had left in the fridge, which he claimed to be a portent of doom. Yes, seriously.)

My mobile phone was on throughout, so my husband could call me from the room where he and baby were stationed should he need me, and a call came through from my home number. It was my mother-in-law telling me that a man had been on the phone saying he knew me and wanting to offer his help.

I recognised his name and immediately excused myself from the meeting to return his call. He was a specialist in distressed finance who had offered me assistance a year earlier, which I eventually did not need to take at the time. He had read the stories in the press and renewed his offer to assist in any way that he could.

I explained the position: that we were in deep problems, and we had submitted an application for the company to have the power to appoint an administrator at court. (This does not put the company into administration; it just prevents anyone else from doing so for two weeks from the date that power is granted, giving the company extra breathing space to find a solution.)

By this point I had to come up with some rock-solid options, rather than vague promises of assistance, so I told him the only way he could help would be by coming up with a cheque for £1million by that afternoon which could be placed in escrow while a deal was done. We had £3 million cash in our bond, much of which was due to be released back to us in August as it related to vouchers which had expired on 31 July, so this money combined with the £1 million now on offer would have been sufficient to allow us to trade through. He told me this was not a problem; he would put up the money short term to allow me to complete the refinancing process which I had begun but which would take three more weeks to complete. If I managed to complete on my deal he would be repaid the money with hefty interest; if I did not achieve it, he would take the majority of the shares in the company in return. It was a last-ditch option, but I just knew that, given a few weeks' breathing space, I could pull it off.

I told him I'd go for it, and then eagerly went back into the meeting room to tell the lawyers and my co-directors that I had found a solution.

I cannot tell you how white the faces of the lawyers in the room went at that point, not to mention the face of the representative from the administrators. I was perhaps naive but I believed that we all wanted to find a way to stop the company going into administration, but as I sat there it dawned on me that they didn't went the same thing. They would only make their fees if the deal went through, and had already persuaded the other directors to sign on the dotted line. A huge amount of time had been invested by that point on a speculative basis, which would only be recovered if the company went into administration. My baby needed feeding, which meant I had to leave the meeting room once more. When I returned to the room I felt like something important had been discussed in my absence. There was sudden talk of directors' responsibilities, for which I'd never heard either of my co-directors show much concern before. The thought then crossed my mind that they, of course, had far less to lose than I, particularly as both stood to continue with the company post-administration and one of them wasn't even a shareholder. Who knows what was said while I was outside the room. Then news came in from the court that our application for the power to appoint an administrator had been overturned, on the basis that a winding-up order had been entered against us the previous Friday. Oh, how creditors can be their own worst enemy in these situations.

By this point, bailiffs were starting to arrive at the company's offices to seize assets, which they are apparently entitled to do if a winding-up order has been granted. The management team had been forced to lock the doors so that no one could get in – which also meant, of course, that none of the staff could get out. My team were now at physical risk, and that is a big responsibility. The only way we could trump the winding-up order, the lawyers told me, was to use the bank's power (they held a debenture over the business) to appoint an administrator. This would protect the business from its creditors while a purchaser was found, which would at least allow the company to remain intact and the staff to keep their jobs.

Drained, emotional and exhausted, and under extreme pressure from all quarters, at 4pm on 1 August 2005 I finally signed my company away. Knowing that if, like Jimmy Goldsmith, I had had just a few days more, things could have turned out very differently.

Hindsight is a very wonderful thing, but if I could have turned back the clock on those last days and months of Red Letter Days, and seeing what saved Jimmy Goldsmith, here is what I would have done differently:

- Brought in the best, top-quality legal advice money could buy, from people that I had utmost confidence in and that wanted the business to survive.
- Removed all 'rogue' directors from the board, ie those with more to gain from seeing the company go through an administration process, than from seeing it survive.
- Kept at least three refinancing options alive and running in parallel.
- Managed the relationship with key creditors personally, rather than leaving this to the finance director (who was, it seems to me, too busy trying to do deals where he would personally profit from the company's downfall, than trying to save it).
- Acted a lot earlier, at the first sign of problems, rather than leaving it until it was too late. You always have less time than you think.

18

EXPECT THE UNEXPECTED

In amongst the 'people'-related business nightmares, it is worth spending a little time looking at the unexpected disaster scenarios which can side-swipe an otherwise perfectly stable and healthy business seemingly overnight. Lots of examples come to mind. The cancer scare which effectively obliterated Perrier water as a brand in the 1980s – at a time when it was far and away the market leader; the bird flu epidemic which took TV cameras inside the workings of Bernard Matthews' turkey farms and put people off eating his products for ever; and the images of Concorde on fire and crashing into a field in France in 2000. This not only inflicted damage on the British Airways brand (even though it was an Air France Concorde that crashed), it also totally decimated the business of the specialist Concorde experience tour operator Goodwood Travel. They were one of Red Letter Days' most well-run experience suppliers, but never really recovered from the disaster, and eventually had to close in 2003 (although the brand has since been revived under new ownership).

You can have well-practised disaster recovery scenarios in place, but even the best-managed businesses cannot always anticipate everything. Also, the modern media moves so fast it can easily leave a business on the back foot when it comes to managing customer perception of your brand.

Of course most of these disasters happen at the most inconvenient time – in the middle of the night or at the weekend when it is difficult to summon the teams you need to manage the situation quickly and effectively. This was the situation that top businesswoman Dawn Gibbins MBE found herself in, in May 1995 when the manufacturing and commercial centre of her business, Flowcrete, was devastated by fire.

Flowcrete is one of the world's leading flooring manufacturers. It was started by Dawn and her father in 1982 when they were commissioned to design a sugar-resistant flooring system for Mars Confectionery. The success of this project resulted in other commissions and soon they were working for NATO, creating infrared-reflecting camouflage coating for airfields. A series of product innovations followed and, each time, the company acquired valuable patents enabling it to market its flooring solutions throughout the UK.

By 1994 sales had reached £3.5million and Dawn was the youngest ever industrialist to be awarded an MBE for services to industry. But a year later disaster struck. A 15-year-old local arsonist built a bonfire adjacent to the fire door of the company's factory and pretty soon the entire building was ablaze.

Dawn recounts the experience: 'I was horse riding in the foothills of the Pennines with my kids and, descending down the hill back home to Congleton, the kids got so excited about a big bonfire they could see in the distance. "Let's go see the fire mum!" they exclaimed. So we stopped at a garage in my local town to buy some naughty things to nibble and drink and asked the attendant where the fire was, and he said "Flowcrete". There was a silence. "Pardon?" I said. "Flowcrete." Another silence. He actually had to repeat it six times for it to sink in that it was actually my own business which was on fire. So I screamed, got the kids in the car and shot to the scene.'

'I was stopped by the police, who offered to look after my kids (then aged five and seven). They loved policemen and police cars, so they were fine. I, however, was not, particularly as by this point the roof had collapsed as the fire brigade had not been approached early enough, and they did not have knowledge of what was inside the building.'

All the company's directors were away for the weekend, leaving just Dawn and her production manager to deal with the crisis. The fire brigade would not go near the building as they thought it might explode, teams of journalists from the local radio and TV stations started to descend on the scene, and the CID even started investigating Dawn for arson (Flowcrete was not in financial trouble at the time, but companies have been known to engineer 'accidents' to generate insurance payouts).

'My initial feelings of shock, horror and total loss soon turned to strength, and I thought, "Right, what can we do, who do I need to call?" That night was spent contacting phone companies, staff and so on. Luckily it was the Sunday of a bank holiday – so I had the Monday to make more calls.'

Dawn immediately focused on getting the business up and running again – phones had to be re-routed, the staff re-housed into new premises, and the bank manager persuaded to extend an overdraft to replenish the stock devastated by the fire. He also had to be persuaded to finance the short-term upheaval while insurance monies were claimed. On top of all the business-related issues, Dawn was even threatened by the local River Authority, who wanted her to restock the entire river's fish population!

Flowcrete was able to withstand the disaster and subsequently launched its products internationally. The company now has a turnover of over £44million, with sales offices in 26 countries and manufacturing plants in the UK, USA, Malaysia, Sweden, Belgium, Brazil and South Africa, winning Dawn the Veuve Clicquot Businesswoman of the Year Award in 2003 as well as numerous other awards and accolades.

Had it not been for Dawn's fast-acting initiatives and hard work in its moment of crisis, the outcome for the company could easily have been so very different. (Sadly, the teenager responsible for the fire was not captured by police and went on to commit a murder before he was finally put behind bars).

I asked Dawn whether the business would now be fully prepared for a similar incident.

'No. I don't think you are ever prepared for it. Yes, we are better equipped and have so much more technology now to set ourselves back up in business – but it still would be a trauma. But we entrepreneurs don't do "negative" – no matter what happens we just rewire ourselves and get positive again. Or should I say we enjoy the challenge? I am always enthusiastic to the point of being obnoxious – so much so that people actually ask me to tone down sometimes!'

Of course, your challenges will vary according to your business and your sector, but it is well worth spending the time brainstorming the 'what if?' scenarios so that when things unexpectedly go wrong, as they always will, you are prepared to cope and, most crucially, your business is in a position to recover.

Here are the lessons that Dawn learned as a result of her business nightmare:

- 'Secure your premises well, including building a big spiky fence to prevent anyone getting close to the building.'
- 'Store important data off-site. My finance manager had kept our back-up discs in a fire safe which actually melted; we had to recreate our accounts from a six-week-old debtors' list and ring our customers and ask what they had purchased during the last month. How embarrassing!'
- 'Ensure that you have up-to-date stock records and asset registers. We had to recreate ours from out of my management team's heads.'
- 'Network with your local business community. It was our local Business Link CEO who was the greatest help – he suggested key premises in the area which he knew were empty for us to move into next day. He was a star.'
- 'Bond with your bank manager early on so he is willing to help, should you encounter a crisis. It is so important to secure extra cash to replenish stock and buy new equipment as soon as possible. Ensure your bank manager has faith in you and your ability.'
- 'Ensure that you have adequate insurance cover, but bear in mind that the money will take a long time to come through.'

19

THE WILDERNESS YEARS

No book on business nightmares could be complete without a mention of Gerald Ratner, whose famous Institute of Directors 'crap' speech was jumped on by the tabloids and effectively destroyed the Ratners jewellery business, which had been founded by his father and uncle.

Much has already been written about the mistakes Gerald made that day: the need to avoid complacency in business; the damage which can be caused to your brand through a single misplaced statement; the impossibility of controlling the British media once they have got hold of a story. But the thing I want to write about in relation to Gerald is the soul-destroying nightmare of surviving the 'wilderness years' that follow a high-profile business meltdown. When I read Gerald's book *The Rise and Fall... and Rise Again* (Capstone, 2007), there were so many parallels with my own experiences following the crash of Red Letter Days that I just had to write about them.

Gerald kindly agreed to allow me to use excerpts from his book, as well as to answer my questions, to enable me to write this chapter.

The sad fact is that, because 99% of the British population don't really do anything particularly remarkable with their lives (tabloid journalists included), when someone does achieve something extraordinary, or create a vast amount of wealth, it creates a huge amount of jealousy. Should that person fall from grace, there are literally millions of people who are more than happy to put the boot in. Most people blindly form their opinions based on what they read in the newspapers, so no one really wants to either know the truth behind the headlines or try to understand the person who has just been shot down. More than that, most people are pretty spineless, and so herd instinct dictates that they will want to distance themselves from the fallen hero, rather than support or defend them in any way. So, if you experience a high-profile crash, apart from close family and friends (and sometimes even they desert you) you are pretty much going to have to get through it alone.

The biggest issue in the aftermath is one of money.

Thanks to all the Rich Lists that are printed these days, you could be forgiven for thinking that all successful entrepreneurs are rolling in money. But what those valuations don't let on is that most of the 'wealth' of an entrepreneur is tied up in the shareholding of the company they run. So remove the company and you remove most of an entrepreneur's net worth. It's not just the capital value that is lost; all of their salary, benefits and expense accounts evaporate too.

It is also inevitable that no matter how much you earn, your expenditure always increases to match it: the luxury executive-sized home you occupy will typically have an accompanying executive-sized mortgage, and your top-of-the-range cars will be either company owned or lease financed. So a decision has to be made very early on: do you downsize, take the kids out of private school and live like a pauper for a while? Or do you quickly find other ways to generate the lost income? In Gerald's case he suffered a slow and painful dissipation of his wealth after making that infamous speech.

Ratners' sales began to dry up (no one wanted to buy products that were 'crap'), and the company had to move from expansion to cost cutting overnight, which included reducing Gerald's yearly salary from £650,000 to £350,000, selling his company-owned London home and withdrawing the use of a number of company-owned cars.

The company's share price was also in free fall and Gerald's Ratners shares – which had once been worth £8million – were now worth only £100,000. And he had tax bills looming.

So he sold his £1.5million home (which at that point had negative equity of £200,000) for one worth £375,000, and even then he had to persuade the bank to loan him £575,000 to fund the transaction.

After a long and painful decline over an 18-month period, the company finally removed him from the board. 'I had worked bloody hard for 30 years, making millions of pounds for shareholders and creating thousands of jobs for a company I loved, and suddenly I had it taken from me. Not for doing anything criminal. I hadn't embezzled. I hadn't lied. All I had done was say a sherry decanter was crap. The pay-off would barely cover my negative equity and the coming year's school fees. I wasn't just unemployed, believe it or not, I was penniless.'

This is where it helps to have a good relationship with your bank. Gerald's helped him out with an overdraft facility and mine cushioned the blow while I sold my Sandhurst home. I was adamant that I would not allow the meltdown of Red Letter Days affect our family's lifestyle, and as an entrepreneur I actually saw the financial void as a bit of a personal challenge.

I remember the day when the sale of our house finally came through a year later (by then we had relocated to Bakewell, where we decided to rent a house until we were in a better position to buy). The sum of £735,000 arrived in my bank account, but once we had paid off our mortgage, loans and overdraft, I was left with precisely £3,184.

The second big issue of being in 'the wilderness' is the way you are treated by those around you. Gerald recalls the day that he was finally removed from the Ratners board:

'That night, unable to make conversation, I flipped on the TV and caught the *News at Ten*. Towards the end of the bulletin there was a short piece on my departure from Ratners. The newsreader also announced that the company's name would be changed. Ratner was now a name that brought embarrassment to everyone who used it, and the group would now be known as Signet.

'Watching your demise on TV is a little like being present at your own funeral – and it isn't something anyone should live to see.'

I identified with that feeling when I think back to the night *Tonight with Trevor MacDonald* featured the crash of Red Letter Days, calling the segment 'Exit the Dragon'. I had declined to be interviewed for the show because it was a pre-record and my PR man knew that whatever I said would be twisted in the editing to fit the story. So I declined and sent a statement to ITV instead – only part of which was broadcast on TV.

To sit and watch people whom I had trusted – my chairman Sir Rodney Walker, a member of my staff whom I had only known for six weeks and one of our 'experience suppliers', for whom I had generated literally millions of pounds' worth of business over the decade I had worked with him – openly slag me off on television was just very, very saddening. Of course I was painted as a complete con-woman who had kept people fooled for years. It was a total stitch-up.

I had made sure that my children were not around while we watched that show – I had told them that I had sold the company. But perhaps the saddest moment of my life was a few days later, when I found my eldest son MJ watching the programme on Sky Digital. He was nine at the time, and had grown up in the Red Letter Days business. I was a single mother when he was born and I used to take him to the office with me all the time. I would work away at my computer while he would play with his toys or scoot around the office in his baby-walker. When the Red Letter Days hot air balloon was launched at a balloon fair in Oxford he was there to proudly see it take off.

I also later discovered that a close 'friend', whom I had invited over to watch the TV programme with me but who declined because she was 'busy', had in fact had a TV 'party' at her house with a few other bitchy friends – clearly gleeful about my downfall. Needless to say, none of them are friends any more.

But that night the most amazing thing also happened. Feeling at rock bottom, I logged on to my email at about 10pm, and was amazed to see messages dropping into my inbox one by one – some from friends but most of them from complete strangers, who had seen the show and who were writing words of support.

Similarly, Gerald experienced the same thing.

'I received several supportive phone calls from people I had met over the years. People found it difficult to know what to say, but their good wishes and encouragement were genuinely soothing. Knowing that not everyone thought I was a complete waste of space was something I needed to hear, especially when I would occasionally receive letters from shareholders and customers telling me what a terrible person I was.

'I was so stunned by what had happened to me that it was impossible to see a way forward. Not only had I lost my job, but I had lost the only job I wanted. When I'd been a little boy, I had wanted to run Ratners. I never had any other ambition. It had consumed my thoughts and my energies for so many years that I had never stopped to think about what I might do afterwards. It was a job I had thought I would have for life. It's difficult to explain, but I felt that I had lost my future, that all the events and milestones I had mapped out for myself had faded. Without the structure and support network – chauffeurs, secretaries, accountants – and a diary full of meetings, my life seemed incredibly empty. Like many men of my generation, I had let myself be defined by my job, and without it, I didn't really know who I was.

'It was my wife who saved me. She started sending me on errands – to pick up something from a shop in Henley or Marlow – and so that I would be out of the house for longer, I cycled. This became my latest obsession, and for the next 15 years, cycling would remain an important part of my life.

'Something physical happens to you when you exercise, you release endorphins that make you feel better. They've been known to numb pain, and that's exactly what I used cycling for. Not only did cycling get me out of the house – often for hours at a time – it blotted out the pain. Other people turn to drink, I turned to exercise.'

I am a great believer that successful businesses are most likely to come out of things that you love doing, and for Gerald it was his new-found health and fitness 'addiction' which led him to the success he desperately needed to rehabilitate both his finances and his self-esteem.

'Health and fitness had become a major force in my life, but the facilities at my gym were really for the ladies-who-lunch set. I decided to employ a personal trainer, which I really couldn't afford, to come to the gym with me. She had put a card through my door, and I thought I would see if it made any difference. She made me work out much harder than I did when I was on my own, and I began to see and feel the improvement.

'Once I had introduced her to my gym, she advertised on the noticeboard there, and pretty quickly landed herself 30 clients at £30 an hour. She was earning £900 per week, and as soon as I had realised that, I knew there was a market for an up-market heath club with state-of-the-art fitness equipment.

'I started telling people who used the club that I wouldn't mind opening my own gym, and one day, one of them told me I should meet a friend of hers. This guy had had the idea of opening a health club for some time and had actually found a site to build one. He was probably 10 years younger than me, about 35, and was clearly hungry for success. I got the feeling we could make a pretty good team.'

A couple of months later his business partner called to say he'd found a site.

'It was the first unit on a new industrial estate, which doesn't sound promising for a luxury health club, but it was just a mile out of town and had plenty of parking. It had one huge benefit: elsewhere on the estate was the headquarters of Perpetual Insurance, and this meant hundreds of potential customers who had nothing but a staff canteen to spend their lunch hour in.

'When I got home, I couldn't stop talking. All of a sudden, something that had been an idle notion for a year or more had become very real to me: I could imagine a club at that location, and my mind went into overdrive thinking about the possibilities the site offered. I imagined a pool, steam rooms, saunas, therapy areas – it was going to be the best health club anyone had ever seen.'

Gerald had got his energy back again, and the club opened in 1997, six years on from the Ratners debacle. Four years later he sold the club for £3.9million. The due diligence dragged on longer than expected, and Gerald started to doubt whether the deal would go through. He and his family had a skiing holiday booked, and couldn't get a refund on it, so they went, with the deal still incomplete. 'At 10 o'clock one night my mobile rang. It was one of my co-owners of the club who said, "Congratulations Gerald, the deal has finally gone through." I'm not quite sure if I screamed, but it felt like the joy inside me just wanted to burst out. This wasn't just a deal that gave me financial security; it was a deal that put the speech and its aftermath behind me.

'It sounds a bit cheesy to say it, but I have made that kind of money before and had never appreciated it. When you've lost a huge amount of money and gone back to square one and made a lot of money again, you really do understand its value.'

It took Gerald a decade to reach that point, and time is a great healer. He used the money from that venture (and his new-found confidence) to go back into the jewellery business. Geraldonline.com was launched in 2004.

'The internet has rewritten the rules of how to run a business. In the 1980s and '90s, there was formality to corporate structures, and it was a status thing to have so many people working for you. Computer systems mean we don't need an entire finance department, and as we don't have thousands of shops, we don't need a facilities team eating into our profits. I don't have a team of staff running after me – the days of a chauffeur and PA have long gone – and I answer my own emails and manage stock levels from a laptop in my garden.

'But it would still give me a huge amount of pleasure to buy back the UK shops Signet still owns. If they ever put those shops up for sale, I will certainly be one of the bidders.

'I still haven't forgiven anyone, although Richard Stott, the editor of the *Daily Mirror* who initiated the 'Crapners' story, died of cancer last year, but it was all so long ago that I was ambivalent. I would probably say to others "time heals all" – although you're never completely healed – but don't give up, because the future is unpredictable. Yes I fear going skint again, and if I could turn the clock back I would become a business recluse as far as the media are concerned.'

On hearing Gerald's nightmare my observation is that men find it far more difficult to deal with a business failure than women. Women can often see the spiritual purpose behind life's unexpected events and learn to forgive and forget, whereas men's egos are far more easily bruised and they experience much more anger, plus in some cases a desire for revenge.

For my part, I am only two and a half years into my own 'wilderness years'. I've used the time to re-invent our family's life by moving from the South-East up to the Peak District, which has to be one of the most beautiful places where you can imagine living. I was lucky enough to have a really supportive husband, and it was actually the stability of his earnings that really helped us through financially. I also had my fifth (and last!) baby in 2007, and for the first time in my life, I gave myself a proper 'maternity leave'.

Thanks to the London property boom, we sold the loft apartment next to the Tate Modern, which was originally our London base, at a phenomenal profit. This allowed us to buy a new £1million home on the hill overlooking Bakewell.

Partly because of *Dragons' Den* and partly through people's morbid curiosity immediately after the Red Letter Days meltdown, I started to get asked to do lots of speaking engagements. Although I was absolutely terrified of public speaking, I was being offered up to £8,000 for an event – which was enough money to force me to face my fears.

As a result, I started to become obsessed with improving my performance and I would pay particular attention to how other people at the conferences I spoke at came across, and tried to incorporate what I saw worked into my own 'act'. I took vocal coaching lessons from a brilliant lady called Alice Tierney, who taught me how to project my voice and deliver my speeches.

I am still not as brilliant at speaking as I would like to be, but there are occasionally those events where the energy of the audience seems just right and I can tell I've moved people with my story. The adrenalin rush of the applause and positive feedback after a good performance reassures me that I am wanted and valued again.

So instead of dreading speaking at events, I now really look forward to them. Speaking, for me, was my saviour, in the same way that cycling was for Gerald.

I now work from home and devote practically all my time to working in the small business sector; inspiring, motivating and helping entrepreneurs achieve business success via my speaking, through mentoring and also in various consultancy projects. I love helping others where I can, although I have learned to say 'no' to the many hundreds of people who now email me wanting lots of free advice and help. This is my business now, and I still need to generate an income. Of course, I am now an author, which is something I had always dreamed of being, but never had the time for when I was running Red Letter Days.

People often ask me when I'm going to run my next 'big business' but I am quite happy to run Rachel Elnaugh Ltd for now. I value my new lifestyle so much that I could not bear to have to devote the sheer amount of time I know, from experience, that it takes to get a huge, multi-million-pound new business off the ground. Plus, of course, I now have another baby to look after. I also cannot imagine doing that horrendous commute into a London head office again.

I am often approached by people who want me to go back into the experiences sector, and I must admit there was a time when I thought about re-acquiring my baby Red Letter Days. But that era has passed and I think that in life you have to move on. So when the time comes, my next 'big business' will be something I can operate from a base in Bakewell. But most important of all, it will be a business which is a force for positive change in the world, rather than being purely a money-making machine.

Here's my advice on how to survive the wilderness years:

- Don't try to get back on the horse straight away. You need to give yourself time to mourn.
- Build as many short-term revenue streams as you possibly can. These will tide you over until you have regained your energy and impetus to achieve your next big success.
- In times of desperate need, don't be ashamed to ask people for help – in the knowledge that the day will come when all favours will be repaid in full.
- Time changes us all; your next success may be in a totally different field to the one it was before. Many highly successful people have changed career at some point in their lives. Keep your mind open to all opportunities.
- A difficult trick to pull off, but try to see your failure as a vital part of your personal growth, which will lead you to a place which is ultimately much more rewarding and fulfilling.
- Use the time to clear out everything else in your life which is no longer working, or which represents the 'old you' – whether that be possessions, friendships, habits or ways of thinking.
- Rather than focusing on everything that you may have lost, focus on the things which you still have. Even if that list only begins with a few things on it (for example, your family and your health), over time living with an 'attitude of gratitude' will help you see that we are all surrounded by the most amazing world of abundance and possibility.
- Remember, in life ultimately there are only two things to worry about: whether you are alive or whether you are dead. If you are alive you have no worries!

20

THE BIGGEST NIGHTMARE OF THEM ALL...

One of the most charismatic entrepreneurs I have ever had the pleasure of meeting is Felix Dennis, the founder of the Dennis Publishing Empire. His book *How To Get Rich* (Ebury Press, 2007) has to be one of the best books on business that I have ever read.

I met Felix on Evan Davis' Radio 4 show *The Bottom Line* in December 2006. We had been brought in along with Bill Jordan (the founder of Jordans Cereals) to discuss trends in business and how failure can be turned to your advantage.

I had read about Felix's book in *The Times*, but had never actually bought it, and so I thought I would buy a copy for myself, plus a few extra for Felix to sign with personalised messages as special Christmas presents for my alpha-male husband, brother and a friend.

It wasn't until the train ride home when I started to read my copy (in which, incidentally, Felix had scrawled 'To Rachel, Go For It!' inside the front cover) that I became enthralled by the story of his entrepreneurial journey.

Felix started out with absolutely nothing – at the age of 25, he was living in a small West End flat where the electricity and gas had been cut off because he couldn't pay the bills, feeding broken furniture he had found in a skip into the open fire just to keep warm.

He had some experience in publishing from working at *OZ* magazine in his early twenties, and he was determined to create his own titles. With absolutely no capital to his name, Felix set up Dennis Publishing simply through calling in favours from friends and acquaintances, and persuading suppliers to back him on the promise of future business. As a result, he retained 100% of the company, which he still owns to this day. He never forgot those early supporters, whom he remained loyal to with his business, and made them all extremely rich men.

His first title, *Cozmic Comics,* barely made a penny, but it was a foundation for more publishing ventures and after two years of slowly building up the business, by 1974 he had £60,000 in the bank. It was then that his big break came.

Kung-fu was the latest craze to hit Britain, and Felix had had the foresight to send a journalist over to Hong Kong at the time of Bruce Lee's death a year before. The journalist had brought back a wealth of photographs, as well as interviews with everyone who had ever known Bruce Lee. The resulting magazine, *Kung Fu Monthly*, was an instant success and continued to be published for the next 10 years. Crucially, immediately after the first issue had proven itself, Felix travelled to country after country to license the title to numerous foreign publishing companies. It was this success that established Dennis Publishing as a serious, if small, specialist UK publisher.

Then, in the early 1980s Felix had the foresight to anticipate the personal computer boom and acquired a title called *Personal Computer World*, into which he poured all his resources, building it into the leading computer magazine of its time. Pretty soon, the title's success came to the attention of the publishing giant EMAP, who approached Felix with an offer of £700,000 to buy it. A considerable sum in those days, and a tempting offer for the financially over-stretched publisher, but boldly Felix refused it. Then, another approach came a few months later, this time from the Dutch publishing company VNU, out of whom, through some shrewd negotiation, Felix audaciously managed to extract £3million for the title.

As a result of his relentless innovation and the ability to negotiate phenomenal deals, by the late 1980s Felix had grown seriously rich. But he was also spending millions on drink, drugs and women. Eventually he was hospitalised and told that unless he changed his lifestyle he would die.

Felix cleaned up his act, started to refocus on building a huge publishing empire and became a workaholic, ruthless in his pursuit of material wealth, pretty much to the exclusion of all else in his life.

By his own admission, Felix writes: 'Making money

was, and still is, fun, but at one time it wreaked chaos on my private life. It consumed my waking hours. It led me to a lifestyle of narcotics, high-class whores, drink and consolatory debauchery. But like an old, punch-drunk boxer, I couldn't quit. I always craved just one more massive payday. One more appearance under the lights with the roar of the crowd and the stink of the sawdust and leather. One more fight. Then I'll retire. Just this last one.

'It's no excuse, but making money is a drug. Up to as recently as 1999 I was still working 12–16 hours a day making money. With hundreds of millions of dollars in assets I could not just let go. Like I said, it was pathetic, because whoever dies with the most toys doesn't win. Real winners are people who know their limits and respect them.

'Riches do not confer happiness! I have lost count of the number of friends, lovers and acquaintances I have told this to, especially when I first passed seven noughts of cash in hand. I don't bother any more. The incredulous look on their face is always the same.'

Felix points out that there are only two things apart from health and love worth fussing about in life. They are time and freedom. Money is only worth having if it is able to buy you these.

'Ask me what I will give you if you could wave a magic wand and give me my youth back. The answer would be everything I own and everything I will ever own.

'If you are young and reading this then I ask you to remember just this: you are richer than anyone older than you, and far richer that those who are much older.

If you are young, you are infinitely richer than I can ever be again.

'The rich are not happy. I have yet to meet a single really rich happy man or woman – and I have met many rich people. The demands from others to share their wealth become so tiresome and so insistent, they nearly always decide they must insulate themselves. Insulation breeds paranoia and arrogance. And loneliness. And rage that you only have so many years left to enjoy rolling in the sand you have piled up.

'Come back to these words in 20 or 30 years, when new books printed on paper will be rare objects. Then cast your mind back to a time when you were young and to the thoughts of a fool, a rich poet, long dead, who once typed these words sitting in one of the most beautiful houses on earth, staring at turquoise sea, sipping a glass of slightly chilled Chateau d'Yquem. That will be enough for me.'

You see, Felix's book is actually not about how to get rich at all. It's about whether you are prepared to pay the terrible price it often takes to achieve great wealth. And I think that is why I love it.

* * *

It's New Year's Day as I write this final chapter. My five boys are with my husband at the other end of the house, having fun, playing with the toys they were given for Christmas while I am in my office trying to finish writing this book.

When I think of all the sacrifices I have made over their short lifetimes, in the relentless pursuit of fortune and fame, I feel almost ashamed. The times I left them in the hands of an army of nannies, childminders, nurseries and au pairs so I could get on with my work. The bitter last few years of Red Letter Days, when I jumped into my little Audi TT roadster each Sunday night and drove up to London to spend the entire week fighting to save the business, only returning to see the children on the Friday night for the weekend. I practically missed my third son's first two years of growing up.

We all know that the reason we work so hard is to provide our children with security and stability, often driven on by fear of what disasters might happen if our toil ever stopped. Most people's reason for wanting to get rich is so that they don't have to work any more. But very few people ever get to that stage, and instead of controlling their business, quickly find that their business starts to control them.

So, if you will excuse me, I am going to stop writing now, and just close by saying, if you find yourself caught up chasing the golden dollar, please give a thought to Felix's words. Because a life spent obsessed with amassing material wealth to the exclusion of all else is surely the biggest nightmare of them all.

A FEW WORDS ON 'ENTREPRENEURIAL ENERGY'

Having spent a year researching for this book, I want to write some words about what I believe to be the single most important ingredient of business success. I don't want to sound negative, but if you don't possess this magic ingredient, your chances of succeeding on your business journey, with all the challenges and potential nightmares you are about to face, are very slim.

There are a million and one books, courses and websites out there which promise to impart this magic secret, but to me the answer is very simple, and it was reinforced during the writing and researching this book. It was clear during my one-to-one interviews with some of Britain's top entrepreneurs, in hearing many speak at business events and as I met many others in my travels over the years. The one thing that all these highly successful entrepreneurs have in common is that they 'vibrate' with a much higher energy than most 'normal' people you meet.

Whether you realise it or not, you're probably pretty good at 'reading' energy. You can walk into a pub or restaurant and instantly feel whether it has a positive, upbeat energy or is 'dead'. Similarly, you know immediately on meeting a friend whether they are 'up' or 'down'. With practice, you can walk into any business – whether it's a shop, a hotel or an office – and know instantly from its energy vibe whether it is doing well, or is struggling and in decline.

Great positive energy is a rare commodity – and it's also highly infectious, which is why motivational speakers (and pop stars) are paid so much and are so hugely in demand. If someone can transform your state so that you walk out of their seminar or concert feeling like you're walking on air, they have injected you with their energy. This simple quality is what turned Anthony Robbins from janitor into the world's richest motivational speaker and Madonna into a phenomenal female pop icon.

Similarly, just spending an hour or so with some of the entrepreneurs I interviewed to write this book charged me with so much positivity I just couldn't wait to scribble all my post-interview thoughts and ideas down. It refreshed me with new impetus and enthusiasm for all of the other business projects I had under way at the time.

When you strip away all the 'Dos and Don'ts' of starting a business, the one inescapable fact is that it takes a *huge* amount of energy (some may call it momentum) to get a new business off the ground. Once you have achieved that momentum, a business quickly becomes very valuable indeed. If you are half-hearted in your approach, lack commitment, don't give it enough of your time (for example, trying to launch your business while still holding down a salaried job full time), or if you possess anything less than 100% enthusiasm for your new business, it simply won't get off the ground.

This is why you'll also find a common theme cropping up in all those great entrepreneurial success stories that you read about – most of them founded a business based on a product or service that they already had an absolute passion for. Failing that, it was sheer passion for money, power and success that drove the others on.

Think about passion for a moment. It's the kind of strong energy closely akin to a highly charged sex drive or to love – both incredibly strong forces in themselves. (On the subject of sex, Napoleon Hill in his classic 1937 book *Think and Grow Rich!* points out that virtually every highly successful person he studied and wrote about – from Napoleon to Henry Ford – had a well-documented, highly developed sex drive.)

The words and phrases used to describe the 'successful entrepreneur' can all be linked back to aspects of the kind of powerful positive energy I am trying to describe – words like charisma, persistence, passion, motivation and determination.

In the Entrepreneurial Profiling Test which I recently created (see page 206), one of the most telling questions is the one where I ask you to describe your personal energy levels. From your answers to that single question I can usually assess immediately whether you have what it takes to 'make it' in business or not.

To get a new business off the ground you need to be working on it almost to the point of obsession – living it, breathing it, thinking about it every moment of the day, probably even dreaming about it! It should be the first thing you think about when you wake up in the morning and the last thing that occupies your mind as you lie in bed at night. You should feel so passionate and highly charged about your business that you can't wait to get back to working on it, can't wait to get out of bed the moment you wake up and get into your office (or shop, or wherever) and get back to progressing it. You should literally be fizzing over with ideas and enthusiasm for it all of the time.

So many budding entrepreneurs I meet or get emails from are so all over the place, chasing a variety of different business projects or ideas, that they spread their energy too thin to be successful at any one thing. This is OK when you are already at the helm of an existing company which has achieved momentum and you are now starting to diversify your portfolio of business interests, but if you are just starting out on your entrepreneurial journey, lack of focus is often the kiss of death.

Napoleon Hill's advice on all this is to sit down and write out your Definite Chief Aim. There is a great example of a Definite Chief Aim, written on a small piece of paper torn out of a textbook by a young Chinese immigrant, which is now framed and hanging on the wall of a Planet Hollywood restaurant in America:

> MY DEFINITE CHIEF AIM
> *I, Bruce Lee, will be the first highest-paid oriental superstar in the United States.*
>
> *In return I will give the most exciting performances and render the best of quality in the*

capacity of an actor. Starting 1970 I will achieve world fame and from then onward till the end of 1980 I will have in my possession $10million.

I will live the way I please and achieve inner harmony and happiness.

Signed Bruce Lee, January 1969

A stunning example of the power of dreams! Bruce Lee made his $10million by 1973 after *Enter the Dragon* was released. Unfortunately no one could have predicted that he would die so tragically later that same year.

The great thing about creating a Definite Chief Aim statement is that it gives a wonderful clarity to your decision making. Every single project you take on or activity that consumes your time or energy is suddenly aligned to your objective.

Not having the focus of a Definite Chief Aim is like having energy scattered everywhere. Even though it seems logical to have lots of 'irons in the fire' at any one time, you will actually dramatically increase your chances of success if you focus on only one thing. It's a bit like concentrating the sun's rays through a magnifying glass. Suddenly, what were just a few warm positive rays of light now have the intensity of energy to start a forest fire.

Having said all of the above, keeping your energy positive and strong is really difficult – especially in the early years when you're trying to get a business off the ground, and especially if you're trying to do it alone from an office at home, with nothing to feed you

Taking responsibility for managing your own motivation is key: how often, when we work in big organisations, do we expect our company to manage our motivation for us?

When problems arise on your business journey – as I'm afraid they inevitably will – keeping your energy positive and highly charged is your best strategy for geting through the crisis unscathed.

Having been in the black hole of depression myself on many occasions, here are my own tips on how to keep your energy levels high:

- Identify and remove any thing (or more usually person!) from your day-to-day business life that regularly brings your energy down. This may sound tough (especially if the problem IS your business or life partner), but it may equally be as simple as painting your office walls a more vibrant colour, replacing an old, slow computer with a new, high-speed one, or removing suppliers who aren't performing or customers who don't pay their invoices on time. Be ruthless and surround yourself only with people and things that make you feel good about yourself, your business, and life in general.
- When you're starting a business you tend to end up spending most of your time on 'output' – reacting, responding, getting things done. So try to get some 'input' for a few hours or even take a day out of the business completely. Try business networking events, an exhibition to give you fresh ideas or a new perspective, or reading a motivational book or entrepreneurial autobiography to help reignite your positivity.
- Constantly work at bringing fresh new energy into the business: new staff, advisers, projects, product lines, anything that makes you more enthusiastic and excited about your business and its future.
- Sluggish energy is usually reflected in clutter. Take a moment right now to look at your office or your workspace. Is it a mess of unruly papers and boxes or things you need to attend to but haven't done? If so, invest a good hour or two in having major sort out. Throw out any clutter and organise what's left – then see how much better you feel about things.

- Watch what you eat and drink. Too much tea and coffee, sweet snacks or even going without eating for hours on end will deplete your energy and stop you being productive. I promise you that even drinking a large glass of pure mineral water right now will have a positive and uplifting effect within just 10 minutes.

- Tackle the difficult jobs once and for all – those ones you've been putting off the ages. That difficult sales call, sorting out the PAYE or VAT, resolving a supplier or staff conflict. Having negative 'undone business' weighing on your subconscious will bring you down.

- Similarly, a mound of unpaid invoices will have a draining and negative effect. Even if there is no money in your bank account to pay them, the act of simply sitting down and writing out the cheques ready to send when money starts flowing (and in the process, working out the size of the total cash you somehow need to generate) will focus your mind back to sales and revenue-generation activity with fresh impetus and energy.

- If you work from home it's easy to spend most of the day in a tracksuit, but making the effort to dress as if you were going for an important business meeting will instantly help raise your spirits if they are starting to flag.

- In the early days, getting sales and cash flowing is the quickest, fastest way to lift your spirits. A new order or a cheque arriving is the biggest indicator of all that you and your product/service are actually in demand and wanted! So spend at least part of every single day focused on sowing the seeds of future sales. The energy you get from a single 'yes' (even if you had to endure 20 'nos' to get there) is often enough to completely recharge your enthusiasm.

- If none of the above works and you're still feeling down, exercise of any sort – even if it is a half-hour break to walk around the block or visit the shops – can be enough to restore your spirits. Whatever works for you.
- Make positive and optimistic thinking your habitual way of life.

CONTACT ME

I spend most of my time these days working in the small business sector, inspiring, motivating and helping others to achieve business success through my speaking, writing, consultancy and mentoring.

I speak at various business events around the UK and beyond about my story and entrepreneurship, and I also now personally run a series of 'entreprenurial masterclasses' – you can find details on my website www.rachelelnaugh.com. I am also continually developing the website to become a source of inspiration and practical advice for entrepreneurs.

Early in 2007 I developed my own unique 'Entrepreneurial Profiling Test' which helps you understand what type of entrepreneur you are and the type of business with which you are most likely to find success. I originally created it as a tool to help me understand the clients who were asking me for help with their businesses, because it is an extremely difficult test to cheat on, and it tells me exactly what makes them tick.

The Test is free for you to take at my website, and will put you into one of 10 different categories of entrepreneur. These are listed overleaf.

TYPES OF ENTREPRENEUR

The Ultrapreneur:

Highly driven, ambitious and visionary, Ultrapreneurs have the potential to become billionaires – as well as ultimately great philanthropists. (James Dyson, Felix Dennis)

The Alphapreneur:

Highly driven by money and the desire to win at all costs, Alphapreneurs are highly competitive and love displaying the trappings of their wealth. (Donald Trump, Peter Jones)

The Passionpreneur:

Passionpreneurs go into business to do the thing that they love, rather than to make money. They have great energy and enthusiasm, and naturally attract the right people and opportunities. (Anita Roddick, Al Gosling)

The Sociopreneur:

Sociopreneurs are driven by a cause and want to use their business to change the world. (Ivan Massow, Emma Harrison)

The Bosspreneur:

As the name suggests, this type of entrepreneur goes into business because they want to call the shots. They like to control everything within their mini-empire and find it difficult to delegate. (Derek Trotter aka 'Del Boy' is the perfect example of a Bosspreneur!)

The Execpreneur:

Execpreneurs typically come from a safe, corporate environment and need structure to function. Often they are specialists who find it difficult to function as good all-rounders and may find it best to work in partnership with others. (Gerald Ratner)

The Lifepreneur:

Lifepreneurs are usually attracted to business because of the freedom of being their own boss, plus often the false lure of making lots of money with less effort than it takes to hold down a full-time job. When they find out that they are working all the hours God sends and it is still difficult to make ends meet, they frequently become disillusioned and give up. (The majority of people fall into this category.)

The Dadpreneur:

Dadpreneurs have typically opted out of the corporate world, creating businesses that give them great flexibility, the ability to work close to home and family, plus real life/work balance. (Most writers and freelancers fit into this category.)

The Mumpreneur:

Lifestyle is all-important for Mumpreneurs, who need to fit their business around their family. They are reluctant to take on risk and often operate their business from home. (Anita Roddick and Laura Tenison both started as Mumpreneurs.)

The Safepreneur:

Safepreneurs are inspired to be in business but when it comes to the crunch often lack the energy and drive it takes to succeed. Risk averse, they are reluctant to leave their salaried job or commit funds to their business. (The entrepreneur type least likely to succeed in business.)

Thousands of people have now taken this test, and because I also ask how many years the person has been in business, I know the types which are statistically more likely to achieve business success (ie those who have survived for more than three years). They are Ultrapreneurs (true business geniuses), Alphapreneurs (highly ambitious and determined), Passionpreneurs (naturally high energy levels), Bosspreneurs (short-term-deal orientated, minimal overhead), Sociopreneurs (driven by deep-seated beliefs and missions) and Dadpreneurs (typically building their business from an existing client base, therefore already having momentum).

The types most likely to fail are Execpreneurs (as they need structure to function and build in too much overhead too early on), Lifepreneurs (who give up when it all seems too much it like hard work), Mumpreneurs (who don't realise just how difficult and time-consuming business can be and distracting from family life) and Safepreneurs (lacking the self-belief and determination to push through problems).

People do travel through the entrepreneur types over time, but your profile will give you an idea where you currently sit on the spectrum. So please do take the test and then write and let me know if it is accurate.

You can always email me at rachel.elnaugh@rachelelnaugh.com. Especially, please write and let me know what you thought of this book. I do personally read every email I receive, and I try to reply whenever time permits.

One of the beautiful things about my current life is that, through the opportunities I have been sent, not least the experience of appearing on BBC TV's *Dragons' Den,* I am now in a position to help others on their entrepreneurial journey. I am also grateful to every person who sent me messages of support and encouragement during my own darkest days, and to those who have written thanking me for the help I have given them, who have all inspired me to pursue this path.

If I can help you in any way, I will. All you have to do is ask. My online business coaching and mentoring is now live online at www.rachelelnaugh.me. In the meantime, I wish you every success, both in business and in life.

ACKNOWLEDGEMENTS

David Lester (founder of the Crimson Business Ltd group that owns Crimson Publishing), who stood by me through the Red Letter Days crash when so many other 'friends' evaporated, and encouraged me to write this book.

Chris West (co-author of *The Beermat Entrepreneur* (Mike Southon and Chris West, Prentice Hall, 2002)), who agreed to review my first few chapters, and gave me the confidence to believe that I could actually become a credible business author.

Louise and Andrew Third at Integra Communications, who believed in me and encouraged me, as well as breathing new life into my PR. The press coverage they have obtained for me has been entirely positive so far, which I believe reflects their integrity and purity of intent.

Holly Bennion and her team at Crimson Publishing, who have shown the utmost patience with me as I struggled to complete this book amongst all my other business and life commitments, and when I deviated from the agreed production schedule time after time.

All those entrepreneurs who agreed to be interviewed or to contribute to this book (including those I interviewed but did not eventually include), when ego could so easily have persuaded them not to participate.

Geoffrey Wansell, for his kind permission to reproduce parts of his book *Tycoon: The Life of James Goldsmith* (Grafton, 1988); Gerald Ratner, for his kind permission to reproduce parts of his book *The Rise and Fall... and Rise Again* (Capstone, 2007); and Felix Dennis, for his kind permission to reproduce parts of his book *How to Get Rich* (Ebury Press, 2007).

My husband Chris, for supporting and encouraging me during the entire process, as well as looking after the kids on numerous occasions when I needed to write.

My lovely boys Mark, Paul, Eddie, Michael and Jack, for putting up with their temperamental and often-absent mum.

And finally, the Adam Street Private Members' Club, London, for the use of their magnificent rooms for the cover photography.

FURTHER READING

The titles I read (or in some cases re-read) during my 'wilderness years' – which gave me the insights and inspiration to write this book:

Against the Odds (James Dyson, Textere Publishing 2000)

Bottled for Business: The Less Gassy Guide to Entrepreneurship (Karan Bilimoria, Capstone 2007)

Business as Unusual (Dame Anita Roddick, Thorsons 2000)

Maverick (Ricardo Semler, Arrow Books 1994)

Tycoon: The Life of James Goldsmith (Geoffrey Wansell, Grafton 1988)

Think Big and Kick Ass (Donald Trump and Bill Zanker, Collins 2007)

The Rise and Fall... and Rise Again (Gerald Ratner, Capstone 2007)

How to Get Rich (Felix Dennis, Ebury Press 2007)

Think and Grow Rich (Napoleon Hill, Marketplace Books 2007)

Purple Cow (Seth Godin, Penguin Books 2005)

Small is the New Big (Seth Godin, Penguin 2006)

Who Moved My Cheese? (Dr Spencer Johnson, GP Putnam's Sons 1997)

The Celestine Prophecy (James Redfield, Warner Books 1994)

Atlas Shrugged (Ayn Rand, Signet 1992)

Out of the Box Marketing (David Abingdon, Thorogood 2005)

Millionaire Upgrade (Richard Parkes Cordock, Capstone 2006)

Walking Tall (Lesley Everett, McGraw-Hill Education 2002)

Freakonomics (Steven D Levitt and Stephen J Dubner, Allen Lane 2005)

The New Philanthropists (Charles Handy, William Heinemann 2006)

Greed and Corporate Failure (Stewart Hamilton and Alicia Micklethwait, Palgrave Macmillan 2006)

The Seed Handbook (Lynne Franks, Hay House 2005)

The Tao of Warren Buffet (Mary Buffet and David Clark, Simon & Schuster 2007)

Good to Great (Jim Collins, Random House 2001)

Blink: The Power of Thinking Without Thinking (Malcolm Gladwell, Allen Lane 2005)

Screw It, Let's Do It (Sir Richard Branson, Virgin Books 2006)

Cosmic Ordering: How to Make Your Dreams Come True (Jonathan Cainer, Collins 2006)

Positively Happy: Cosmic Ways to Change Your Life (Noel Edmonds, Vermilion 2006)

The Secret DVD (www.thesecret.tv, 2006)

Ask and It Is Given (Esther and Jerry Hicks, Hay House 2005)